WHERE EVERYBODY KNOWS YOUR NAME

The definitive book about everyone's favorite television show...

OTHER PIONEER BOOKS

•THE MAGICAL MICHAEL JACKSON
Edited by Hal Schuster. March, 1990. $9.95, ISBN#1-55698-235-6
•FISTS OF FURY: THE FILMS OF BRUCE LEE
Written by Edward Gross. March, 1990. $14.95, ISBN #1-55698-233-X
•WHO WAS THAT MASKED MAN?
Written by James Van Hise. March, 1990. $14.95, ISBN #1-55698-227-5
•PAUL MCCARTNEY: 20 YEARS ON HIS OWN
Written by Edward Gross. February, 1990. $9.95, ISBN #1-55698-263-1
•THE DARK SHADOWS TRIBUTE BOOK
Written by Edward Gross and James Van Hise. February, 1990. $14.95, ISBN#1-55698-234-8
•THE UNOFFICIAL TALE OF BEAUTY AND THE BEAST, 2nd
Edition
Written by Edward Gross. $14.95, 164 pages, ISBN #1-55698-261-5
•TREK: THE LOST YEARS
Written by Edward Gross. $12.95, 128 pages, ISBN #1-55698-220-8
•THE TREK ENCYCLOPEDIA
Written by John Peel. $19.95, 368 pages, ISBN#1-55698-205-4
•HOW TO DRAW ART FOR COMIC BOOKS
Written by James Van Hise. $14.95, 160 pages, ISBN#1-55698-254-2
•THE TREK CREW BOOK
Written by James Van Hise. $9.95, 112 pages, ISBN#1-55698-256-9
•THE OFFICIAL PHANTOM SUNDAYS
Written by Lee Falk. $14.95, 128 pages, ISBN#1-55698-250-X
•BLONDIE & DAGWOOD: AMERICA'S FAVORITE FAMILY
Written by Dean Young. $6.95, 132 pages, ISBN#1-55698-222-4
•THE DOCTOR AND THE ENTERPRISE
Written by Jean Airey. $9.95, 136 pages, ISBN#1-55698-218-6
•THE MAKING OF THE NEXT GENERATION
Written by Edward Gross. $14.95, 128 pages, ISBN#1-55698-219-4
•THE MANDRAKE SUNDAYS
Written by Lee Falk. $12.95, 104 pages, ISBN#1-55698-216-X
•BATMANIA
Written by James Van Hise. $14.95, 176 pages, ISBN#1-55698-252-6
•GUNSMOKE
Written by John Peel. $14.95, 204 pages, ISBN#1-55698-221-6
•ELVIS-THE MOVIES: THE MAGIC LIVES ON
Written by Hal Schuster. $14.95, ISBN#1-55698-223-2
•STILL ODD AFTER ALL THESE YEARS: ODD COUPLE COMPANION.
Written by Edward Gross. $12.95, 132 pages, ISBN#1-55698-224-0
•SECRET FILE: THE UNOFFICIAL MAKING OF A WISEGUY
Written by Edward Gross. $14.95, 164 pages, ISBN#1-55698-261-5

WHERE EVERYBODY KNOWS YOUR NAME

Cheers

BY JAMES VAN HISE

Books for the entertainment buyer

PIONEER

Designed and Edited by Hal Schuster with the assistance of David Lessnick

Library of Congress Cataloging-in-Publication Data
James Van Hise, 1949—
   Cheers: Where Everybody Knows Your Name, The Unofficial Story

   1.   Cheers: Where Everybody Knows Your Name, The Unofficial Story (television)
 I. Title

Published by Pioneer Books, Inc., 5715 N. Balsam Rd., Las Vegas, NV, 89130.

First Printing, 1992

JAMES VAN HISE writes about film, television and comic book history. He has written numerous books on these subjects, including BATMANIA, HORROR IN THE 80S, THE TREK CREW BOOK, STEPHEN KING & CLIVE BARKER: THE ILLUSTRATED GUIDE TO THE MASTERS OF THE MACABRE and HOW TO DRAW ART FOR COMIC BOOKS: LESSONS FROM THE MASTERS. He is the publisher of MIDNIGHT GRAFFITI, in which he has run previously unpublished stories by Stephen King and Harlan Ellison. Van Hise resides in San Diego along with his wife, horses and various other animals.

CONTENTS

INTRODUCTION: A look at the creation of Cheers, its rocky start, and its successes, past and present — **8**

PATRONS: The talented actors behind the beloved characters revealed — **10**

TED DANSON (Sam Malone)	12
SHELLY LONG (Diane Chambers)	18
KIRSTIE ALLEY (Rebecca Howe)	22
WOODY HARRELSON (Woody Boyd)	28
RHEA PERLMAN (Carla Lupozone Tortelli LeBec)	32
GEORGE WENDT (Norm Peterson)	36
JOHN RATZENBERGER (Cliff Clavin)	42
KELSEY GRAMMER (Dr. Frasier Crane)	46
BEBE NEUWIRTH (Dr. Lilith Sternin-Crane)	50

STORIES: A look back at the first nine years, and more — **52**

SEASON ONE (1982-83)	54
SEASON TWO (1983-84)	62
SEASON THREE (1984-85)	70
SEASON FOUR (1985-86)	78
SEASON FIVE (1986-87)	86
SEASON SIX (1987-88)	94
SEASON SEVEN (1988-89)	104
SEASON EIGHT (1989-90)	112
SEASON NINE (1990-91)	120

THE FUTURE: SEASON TEN (1991- in progress) — **128**

INTRODUCTION

The concept was a bar. After all, it had worked before in one of the most popular radio programs of the 1930s, *Duffy's Tavern*. *Duffy's Tavern* was created by Broadway playwright Abe Burrows, the father of James Burrows, who, with Glen and Les Charles, created the hit television series *Taxi*. (The elder Burrows penned such notable Broadway successes as *How To Succeed In Business Without Really Trying* and *Guys and Dolls*.) But his father's radio show was not the real inspiration for *Cheers*, although it may have suggested the setting for the series. The real inspiration was John Cleese's British comedy series, *Fawlty Towers*. (Fittingly, John Cleese played a marriage counsellor on an episode of *Cheers*— who declared that Sam Malone and Diane Chambers were obviously the worst-matched couple that he had ever seen in his entire life!) A direct adaptation of that show (starring Bea Arthur) was a dismal failure. However, what Burrows appropriated was not the characters and setting of *Fawlty Towers*, but rather the fast-paced, wacky and skewed interactions between a group of characters drawn to a bar called Cheers.

Development money from NBC and Paramount came easy because this was slated a soundstage show with no location shooting and a cast of unknowns. Unfortunately, *Cheers* ' premiere on September 30, 1982, produced mixed results: The critics loved it but demographically, the show literally had no audience. It placed consistently in the bottom five shows during almost any given week. In fact, NBC's popular *Hill Street Blues* may have actually been losing viewers due to the weak lead-in provided by *Cheers*.

Things picked up when the show's casting director, Steven Kolzak, located a celebrity guest star for the show— and a most unlikely one at that. Kolzak's mother had long been the personal secretary to Congressman Tip O'Neill, then in the midst of his long tenure as Speaker of the House. It was through his mother that Kolzak learned that O'Neill liked the show. His remark, "Imagine me down at the other end of a bar, drinking a beer with that fat guy," proved to be a prophetic utterance, as one of America's most prominent political leaders soon found himself sharing a brew with Norm Peterson (George Wendt) and the other *Cheers* regulars.

Needless to say, O'Neill's appearance piqued the interest of television viewers across the nation, and *Cheers* rose to the mid-range of the ratings overnight. This was not a totally solid sinecure with the network, but then, it didn't hurt that Grant Tinker (the network chairman) and Brandon Tartikoff (the whiz-kid programming genius) enjoyed the show. And Tinker was the man who brought the Burrows/Charles/Charles gem *Taxi* over to NBC when ABC cancelled it. Despite its shaky ratings position, *Cheers* was picked up for a second season. But the show's fate was hanging in the balance. More people had to start watching it, or it was doomed to be another obscure footnote to television history. (Like *The Tortellis*, a short-lived spinoff of *Cheers*.) Cast members hit the road, and the talk-show circuit, to promote the series. But what really got the ball rolling was the chemistry between Sam and Diane, which itself grew from the chemistry between Ted Danson and Shelley Long. In the long view, it's obvious that *Cheers* owes its real success to the oldest of pastimes: sex.

While Sam Malone leers at every pretty woman who comes in view, the show itself avoids a leering tone. Instead, it presents a clear-eyed, comedic view of the realities of sexual politics— and the ambivalence and changeability that often accompanies a strong sexual attraction. *Cheers* is certainly not a Noel Coward drawing-room comedy (despite Diane Chambers' efforts to the contrary). Nor is it particularly lowbrow (a term recently redefined by the Fox Network's *Married With Children*, which one suspects might be a show Sam Malone would really enjoy— and which Woody Boyd wouldn't get). In essence, it stakes out a middle ground. . . or perhaps a slightly elevated viewing point from which it could watch, with high-powered binoculars, the absurdities of Sam and Diane's faltering mating dance.

Perhaps, in the end, it is its overarching fairness that won it a place in the hearts of the nation's television audience: for what could be more fair than a show which admits that both sexes, men and women alike, are capable of being complete idiots in their pursuit (and/or avoidance) of each other? Whatever the reason, *Cheers* reached the top ten by the time its episodes were being rebroadcast during the summer rerun season. Amazingly, when the Emmys came around, *Cheers* wiped out the competition— even *M*A*S*H** in its final season. It swept Best Comedy, Best Writing (the Charles brothers), Best Director (James Burrows), Best Actress (Shelley Long)— even Best Opening Credits, which was remarkable considering the conventional wisdom that a show's opening credits should feature pictures of the show's stars (*Cheers* never has). From its shaky beginnings, *Cheers* became an (almost) overnight success, and has remained a top ratings contender right on up to the present time.

—BRENT OLIVER

PATRONS

CHEERS is an ensemble show. Relationships between the major characters change. The interactions between the regulars create both the humor and the drama. They make Cheers a place the viewer returns to each week to catch up on the latest doings of his or her friends.

Front row, left to right: John Ratzenberger, Kelsey Grammer, Bebe Neuwirth, Kirstie Alley, George Wendt

Back row, left to right: Woody Harrelson, Ted Danson, Rhea Perlman

TED DANSON (SAM MALONE)

*B*efore the history of *Cheers* unfolded on television, Sam Malone had a checkered past. A Red Sox pitcher laid low by alcoholism, Sam eventually got his act together, and, with a logic only to be found in the situation comedy universe, opens a bar: Cheers. How on earth is a recovering alcoholic going to keep on the straight and narrow while running a bar? Simple for Sam: he channels his energy into the pursuit of the fairer sex with all the drive and motivation he once devoted to his old sport. In fact, the opposite sex is obviously his new sport— and his new dependency. Little did he suspect the changes that would enter his life when Diane Chambers entered the door of his establishment for the very first time, in the first episode of *Cheers*.

This is not to suggest that, even at the height of his involvement with Diane, Sam did not have an eye for other women. Never a complete lothario (only ninety-nine per cent), he has a rule against sleeping with married women. However, there's not much he can do if he doesn't *know* a woman is married. His luck is not always that bad. Sometimes he merely falls for a pyromaniac, or a woman who Diane recognizes as the most suicidal member of her therapy group. As for Diane, whenever things seem to start to heat up with Sam and her, something invariably pops up to confound matters, such as an egomaniacal painter who sweeps her off her feet and convinces her that Sam is an unsophisticated lout— or her psychiatrist, with whom she has an affair and almost marries. When that falls through, it seems certain that Sam will finally succeed with Diane— until he falls for an aspiring woman politician, Janet Eldridge. But his attraction for Diane Chambers finally wins out, and he abandons his new paramour for his true love.

Theirs was a rocky romance, to be certain, ultimately veering close to marriage, only to end abruptly when the flighty Ms. Chambers broke it off and disappeared into the world at large. Disillusioned, Sam sold the bar to a major corporation, bought a boat, and started off on his own around-the-globe voyage. As luck would have it, his boat sank and he drifted ashore in Boston. Sam finds his way back to the bar he once owned and takes a job as bartender. There, he becomes involved in another dance with a woman who is more than his match: Rebecca Howe.

From the start, Sam seems determined to have his way with Rebecca. Perhaps it's a power struggle; she is, after all, his new boss. Along the way, he fights off the advances of Lilith Sternin, but his main focus is clear. Rebecca's overwhelming lack of desire for him is no impediment— but whenever an opportunity arises, his conscience gets the best of him, as when she promises to sleep with him if he catches her smoking. . . which he does. This becomes a repeating pattern with Sam and Rebecca. He *could* have her on a number of occasions, but it never seems quite right. Perhaps there's a decent guy lurking behind Sam's lecherous façade after all.

The power structure is radically altered at Cheers when Rebecca is fired and Sam is hired to replace her, only to arrange for her to be rehired as a waitress. His libido is dampened, however, by the possibility that he may have made an old girlfriend pregnant, and he takes a vow of chastity which he swears to uphold for a year even when the truth exonerates him. Of course, how long can *that* last?

Another opportunity at Rebecca arises when she gets Sam to pretend to be her lover in order to repulse her boss' sexual advances, but again, Sammy proves too chivalrous for his own good. He is further stymied by her romance with the manipulative billionaire Robin Colcord, who arrives on the scene just as Sam begins to realize his own true feelings for Rebecca. Another dance begins, as Rebecca is torn between two prospective partners. For once, Sam seizes the initiative, turning Colcord after discovering that he's breaking the law. The company, grateful, sells Cheers back to Sam for one dollar. This doesn't get him anywhere with Rebecca, until she turns to him for comfort, but she just as quickly turns back to the imprisoned Colcord. When Colcord is finally out of the picture, its anybody's guess what will happen next. But when Sam, after babysitting for Frasier and Lilith, expresses an interest in becoming a father, Rebecca volunteers to help him out! And so, as ever, the convoluted love life of Sam Malone serves as the central focus of *Cheers*.

Ted Danson, who portrays Cheers' womanizing, ex-baseball star, bartender Sam Malone, was born in December 1949, as Edward Bridge Danson III. Educated in Arizona and Connecticut, he started his acting career on stage, eventually finding roles in soap operas (*The Doctors* and *Somerset*, both now off the air)and in commercials. Danson muses, "You never get to be known for what you want to be known for. People always come up and say, 'Hey, weren't you in that lemon chiffon commercial?'" He played a box of cake mix in the advertisement in question.

Danson's film debut was in *The Onion Field*, where he portrayed the bagpipe-playing policeman who becomes killer James Woods' victim. Appearances on such series as *Magnum P.I.* and *Laverne and Shirley* soon gave way to more film roles. First, as the tap-dancing assistant D.A. opposite William Hurt and Kathleen Turner in *Body Heat*. (Kirstie Alley, later his co-star on *Cheers*, almost got the Kathleen Turner role.) Later he landed a role as a vengeful, waterlogged zombie in a segment of the George Romero/Stephen King collaboration, *Creepshow*.

Danson's youth was spent in Flagstaff, Arizona (his father was an archaeologist), and his education took him to Stanford University, where he eventually dropped out, citing the distraction caused by young women students as a primary factor. An ill-fated marriage to a university girlfriend ended after five years.

In 1976, while still working his way up from the stage, commercial, and soap opera treadmill in New York City, Danson met his future wife Casey Coates at an est seminar. They moved to Los Angeles after marrying in 1977, and Danson's career began to look bright.

Shortly after his breakthrough role in *The Onion Field*, however, Danson's wife Casey suffered a stroke while delivering their daughter Kate on Christmas Eve 1979.half of her body was left paralyzed (Kate was unaffected by the stroke.) Danson dropped everything to stay by his wife's side and to take care of their child as well. "I would have looked to /Casey to do it [the child care] had the situation been different." Danson recalled: "It was horrifying. But after you get over the shock, you roll up your sleeves and work at getting things better."

This was a very difficult time for the Dansons, but strength and humor carried them through; a running bet involved who would crawl first, the mother or the child. "Kate won at eight months," noted Casey in an interview in the early 1980's, just as Ted's *Cheers* career was picking up steam. "I still can't stretch my toes or dance, but those are minor problems compared with not being able to lift my arm or hold my baby or hug my husband. . . A relationship changes when you have a baby. The changes just got retarded in our case. It was sheer survival. You don't think about your sex life when you're paralyzed."

There was some friction during this period. Danson recollected the stressful times: "There was a huge rift between us. . . a massive lack of trust. Her gratitude fed into the sense of sacrifice I was feeling.

"My commitment and depth of love for her are sure a lot richer," he was quick to add.

In time, Casey slowly began to regain control of her body, and has since recovered completely. (A second daughter, Alexis, was adopted four years later.)

In 1982, Danson's big break came when he beat out such competitors as William Devane and Fred Dryer for the role of Sam Malone. Ironically, sports, the second (or third) central passion of Malone's life, did not play much of a part in Danson's scheme of things, and he only attended his first baseball game nearly a month into *Cheers'* first season. Sam's cad-like attributes are not drawn from Danson's own personality; in fact, the thoughtful Danson seems more like the sort of man Diane Chambers would have been well matched with.

But even so, tension often flared between Danson and Shelley Long during her five year tenure on the show, although Danson insists that they maintained a professional attitude throughout.

He also continued to work in films, but none of his projects, including *Just Between Friends, Little Treasure, A Fine Mess* and *Cousins* (a remake of the French film *Cousin, Cousine*), did much to gain him a steady foothold in motion pictures, although he was well received for such TV-movie roles as the incestuous father in *Something About Amelia* in 1984 and as a reporter in famine-ravaged Ethiopia in *We Are The Children* in 1987. (With the success of Cheers still a pipe dream at the time of A Fine Mess, one critic commented that Danson was '. . . likely to discover how short the road can be back to underarm deodorant commercials.' Fortunately, Danson's career was headed in the opposite direction, despite whatever unkind critics had to say.)

1987 also brought his breakthrough movie role in yet another American remake of a French hit: *Three Men And A Baby*. Directed by Leonard Nimoy of *Star Trek* fame, this project turned out to be the top-grossing film of all time, and carved a niche in film for three television performers: Danson, Nimoy, and Tom Selleck, late of *Magnum, P.I.* The sequel, *Three Men and A Little Lady*, continued the success. Danson was a bit nervous about working with a star like Tom Selleck: "I had just started to lose a little hair on top and had never noticed it until Tom and I filmed this overhead shot. It's amazing standing next to Tom Selleck. All your little insecurities come welling to the forefront!"

In 1987 Danson faced another challenge: he had to develop a working chemistry with a new female lead after Shelley Long left *Cheers* at the end of its fifth season. His low-key parting words to Diane Chambers were themselves a great piece of acting-in-miniature, but the new *Cheers* needed him to be bigger and brasher than ever. At a farewell party for Shelley Long, Danson toasted her: "I will miss my partner very much." Then he quipped, "After the show I dropped by her dressing room. We made love. . . our spouses are very lenient!" But the heavy question at the time was: how lenient would *Cheers* fans be when faced with a Diane-less *Cheers*?

Fortunately, Ted Danson's new co-star was to turn out to be Kirstie Alley, who, despite a career based in dramatic roles, proved to be a superb comic actress with a style all her own, and the series did not die a sudden death; instead, it maintained and improved upon its place in the ratings, thanks in large part to its central performer, Ted Danson.

Danson, now in his early forties, wears a hairpiece while playing Sam Malone, but goes *au naturel* when he's not working. Somewhat amused, but annoyed, by a New York street poster series "outing" such allegedly bald performers as himself and William Shatner by airbrushing their photos down to the Yul Brynner look, Danson boldly lowered his head during a recent Tonight Show appearance in order to reveal to millions of viewers the full extent of the bald patch on top of his head.It comes nowhere near the bareness of the Danson portrayed on the doctored posters, whose admittedly humorous intent is drastically undercut by the fact that Danson (like the considerably balder Sean Connery) only disguises his hair loss when it is called for by the professional demands of a role.

In a more serious vein, Danson is actively involved in environmental concerns; in addition to donating money, he takes a hands-on approach to the problem, and is personally involved in the day-to-day details of addressing this important issue. Conscience-easing at a distance just isn't his style, and he and wife Casey are founders of the American Oceans Campaign (established 1987), which focuses on coastal resource issues.

Kirstie Alley has commented of Danson: "He's real easygoing and easy to be around. He's goofy. It's very hard for me to be around actors who take themselves really seriously. Ted's not like that at all. He's very funny, and that makes him sexy. And he's a very good kisser."

On the other hand, Danson's wife Casey contends that there is practically no relation between Ted Danson and his television character, Sam Malone. "He usually plays womanizing men," she points out, "and that's the last thing he ever was. Ted says, 'I was born married!'"

Danson concurred. "I consider myself a family man, partially because my parents did it so damned well."

John Ratzenberger attributes a great deal of the success of Cheers to star Ted Danson's easy-going manner. "Ted keeps everybody's sanity," points out Ratzenberger. "He absorbs the angst."

Danson himself is self-effacing about his work. "I have real trouble looking at my work and saying, 'Gosh, that's great.'" On the other hand, he can joke about having his picture on the cover of a well-known national magazine. "I'm going to turn this [magazine] over. This is very distracting. I get lost in that face. . . I haven't spent enough mirror time today."

The Danson family lives in Brentwood, California. A pool is one of the main features of their estate. "it has nothing to do with the fact that we're snotty, rich people. Nothing to do with that." But more seriously, Danson admits, "The reason for the pool is so we can get our exercise year round."

"Swimming is one of the few aerobic exercises I can do," points out Casey. "The thing is, we're not living this Hollywood life. It's about picking up the Cheerios and macaroni from underneath the kitchen bench. We're about never wearing anything you can't throw in the washing machine."

Finally, Danson describes his marriage in a nutshell. "I'm English and she's Greek. Did you ever see *Zorba*? Well, I'm Alan Bates and she's Anthony Quinn."

Danson has not yet commented on his future with *Cheers* beyond the tenth season, but there seems to be a good chance that he will return to portray Sam Malone for an eleventh year at the very least.

SHELLEY LONG (DIANE CHAMBERS)

It all began when Diane Chambers was dumped by her lover Sumner Sloane; distraught, she accepted a job at Sam Malone's bar, strictly to observe the behavior of the inhabitants, of course. She stayed for five years. Possessed of a strange sensitivity, Diane could become upset when a divinity student was attracted to her and thought about giving up his commitment to god— or when Elizabeth Barrett Browning, her beloved cat, passed away. Her life was always complicated, as when she was set up with a date with Andy— who turned out to be a paroled murderer. And through all this, there was the growing awareness of a smoldering fire growing between her and Sam Malone. True, she was distracted, briefly, by his brother Derek. She almost married Sam early on, albeit temporarily, but that was only to assure that her mother received everything in her father's will, and the plan was abandoned as soon as a loophole was discovered.

Diane could be overwhelmed by Andy's sincere efforts to become an actor— even though this led to her nearly being strangled by him in a scene from Othello. Fresh from this, she could easily make a fool of herself trying to impress Dick Cavett, who was unfortunate enough to walk into Cheers while she was on duty. Diane could veer from one extreme to another, planning to marry her psychiatrist only to abandon him to enter a convent. Returning to Cheers, she began to get involved with Sam again, until the two seemed destined to wed. But after a sojourn in a Buddhist monastery, her life took another reeling tangential turn, and she walked out of Sam's life, planning to write her brilliant novel first, instead of marrying him.

Shelley Long, a product of Fort Wayne, Indiana, portrays intellectual-turned-barmaid Diane Chambers. She brought a fresh new ingredient to television sitcoms when *Cheers* debuted in 1982: intelligence. True, Diane herself may not have been quite the savant she believed herself to be, often getting tangled up in her own intellectual web, but it took Shelley Long's brains to bring Diane's foibles and contradictions to life. When things began, in their own confusing way, to heat up between Sam and Diane, Shelley Long became an integral part of what was then America's most-watched romance (or reasonable facsimile thereof).

Not surprisingly, Long's parents were both teachers who wanted her to follow in their footsteps. But Long cut her college career short, and pursued a dual career in acting and modelling after leaving Northwestern University. In Chicago, she became a member of the celebrated Second City comedy troupe, in addition to writing, producing and co-hosting a popular Chicago magazine program known as *Sorting It Out*, for which she won three local Emmys. Her Second City connection led to a television special called *That Thing On ABC*, as well as a move, in the late 1970s, to Los Angeles. The move to Los Angeles led to roles in such films as *A Small Circle of Friends, Night Shift* (with Henry Winkler and Michael Keaton), *Losin' It* (with Tom Cruise) and *Caveman*, wherein she portrayed Ringo Starr's girlfriend, as well as parts on television shows such as *Family* and *The Love Boat*.

Shelley Long met her second husband, Bruce Tyson, on a blind date in 1979. It seems that Tyson had won a dinner for four, and the couple he invited along brought Shelley along to round out the party; they were married in 1981. (Long declines to discuss her first marriage.)

Cheers proved to be the show that made her career, but this was not apparent until the end of the show's shaky first season, when the show's ratings skyrocketed and Long found herself the recipient of an Emmy for Best Actress in a Comedy Series.

Laughs and joshing were prevalent, off camera, on the *Cheers* set, which certainly made the onscreen camaraderie more convincing. Rehearsals often had their own moments that never made it to the screen. After one exchange, where Diane asks Sam, "Is it so hard to tell you you love me?" and Sam replies, "Right now, its damn near impossible," the actors walked off for a break, and Shelley Long got stuck behind a piece of scenery, and soon began to ask for assistance. When a stage crew member finally got started on releasing her, Ted Danson wasn't sure it was such a good idea. "Hey guys, lets think about this!"

In fact, rumors about tension on the Cheers set— specifically between Danson and Long— began to circulate some time before Shelley Long left the show. "That is not a happy set," another studio's producer was heard to say. Sour grapes? *Cheers* was, after all, one of the top-rated shows of the period in question. And Ted Danson declined to fuel any rumors. "I ain't gonna say anything bad about my partner. I mean, my wife and I have terrible arguments sometimes, and they're kind of our business. Our relationship, Shelley's and mine, has included not being happy with each other and being happy with each other."

Long's own comments seemed to defuse any rumors of discord, which were probably blown out of proportion by the tabloids anyway. "We did our jobs with a caring for each other. That doesn't mean that there weren't days that were harder than others.

"Terrible teasing went on in the relationship and outside the relationship, but our energy went into our work and it paid off."

When Long announced her plans to leave the show, public response was strong. "Sometimes people treat me like I'm going to die," she observed at the time. Oddly enough, Shelley Long's departure coincided with the show's seemingly inexorable drive towards a Diane Chambers/Sam Malone wedding— and the wedding was her idea. "Ted and I walked into the middle of a writing session, and I don't think we've done that more than once or twice in five years." She and Danson wanted to know when their characters would finally get around to tying the knot. But by the time the season was nearing its end— and the expiration of her contract— she realized that it was over. "It wasn't until [then] that I realized it was going to be hard to say goodbye."

Finally, director James Burrows told her that she had to make a decision so that they could plot the rest of the season. (Ted Danson had already signed on for another year, at least.) She admitted, "Okay, I've been procrastinating because I am not looking forward to this." She arranged a meeting with *Cheers'* producers and also requested that Ted Danson attend the meeting. "Ted said later that was his clue that I wasn't going to do it. I said, 'Really? I would have wanted you there even if I'd said I do another year. . . I knew that it needed to be said and without a lot of words. So I just declared, 'I have decided that this will be my last season with *Cheers.*'"

In retrospect, she observed the effect that playing Diane Chambers had had on her life: "My vocabulary has increased tremendously. After five years, there aren't too many words that Diane hasn't said. . . every time you [asked] her a question, [you'd] get a paragraph."

At the party following the shooting of Shelley Long's final scene on Cheers, cast and crew held a party. "They put together a lovely piece of footage of just the Diane character, which was very nostalgic," recalled Ted Danson. "We realized just how much we had done together over these past years." His toast was simple but eloquent: "I will miss my partner very much."

Long's penultimate season with *Cheers* was complicated by the fact that she was pregnant by her stockbroker husband Bruce Tyson; camera angles concealed the fact, an approach avoided by co-star Rhea Perlman, whose character Carla became pregnant also. Long gave birth to a daughter, Juliana. (A post-departure guest appearance as Diane Chambers was at one point considered, but was dropped when a tragic miscarriage disrupted Long's life— a fact she courageously announced herself in order to avoid any "scoops" by the tabloids.)

Long starred in one film while still working on *Cheers, The Money Pit*, and has since been in such movies as *Irreconcilable Differences, Troop Beverly Hills, Hello Again*, and *Outrageous Fortune* (with Bette Midler).

Bette Midler observes of Long: "Shelley has an old-fashioned quality that studio people used to have. She has a very pretty speaking voice and she has a lot of personal dignity."

Long herself was pleased to have made the move to the big screen. "Movies seem to be opening up to me now, and I want to take advantage of that," she stated around the time of her departure from *Cheers*. "I've already crossed the road. I mean, I've made a choice. *Cheers* will do just fine without me."

"It's time to move into the next phase. I've studied the [*Cheers*] question carefully because I knew that was only fair to me and the *Cheers* people and the fans. I know many of them have made their displeasure known. People who work on the show have said their friends told them, 'You tell Shelley that we're really disappointed. And I feel bad because it's going to be hard not to see Diane with Sam. Did I say this already? *Cheers* will do just fine without me."

Although her film career has not reached the heights she achieved on television, her work is still top-notch (although some of her project choices have been otherwise). Sadly, a possible *Cheers* guest appearance by Diane Chambers fell through when Long's life was disrupted by a tragic miscarriage; Long made this public herself, so as to keep the tabloids from "scooping" the story and violating her privacy. (She did appear on the anniversary special with John McLaughlin, however.) Still, the future is an open book for Shelley Long, whose fine-tuned comedic timing should certainly keep her busy in the future. And who knows? Maybe when *Cheers* ends its final season, and Sam Malone is reeling from yet another strange reversal of fortune. . .maybe that door will swing open, revealing the mystery of what Diane Chambers has been doing with herself all these years.

KIRSTIE ALLEY (REBECCA HOWE)

She was already there when Sam Malone returned, and Rebecca Howe already knew about his lecherous ways. There was no way *she* would ever succumb. In fact, at first she seemed made of the most impenetrable ice; but soon enough, the warmth (and confusion) of the woman began to show through. In fact, rumors soon surfaced that she'd been pretty wild in her college days— much to her embarrassment. The truth was, she was in a fairly iffy position in her corporation, and needed desperately to prove herself. To complicate matters, she had a tendency to fall for men in power, such as her boss Evan Drake, perhaps in the hope of rising to the top with his assistance— not that she'd ever admit that to herself. But why else would she sneak into his bedroom while he was out of town? The trapping of power hold their own special allure for Rebecca Howe. But her efforts to ensnare Drake seemed doomed. All her moves were wrong. It was bad enough when the girl she was jealous of turned out to be Drake's daughter, but she had to break the young lady's jaw! Her efforts to quit smoking didn't go much better, either. In an attempt at aversion therapy, she promised to sleep with Sam Malone if he caught her smoking, only to be caught in her own promise. (In a strange lapse, however, Sam acted the gentleman— only to kick himself later.) Her final efforts to grab Evan Drake, on his way to Tokyo with his girlfriend, only landed her in jail, to be bailed out by Sam.

In a company shakeup, Rebecca is fired. Her replacement is, gallingly, Sam Malone, who helps her get a job at Cheers again— as a cocktail waitress.

When she dates a company executive in an effort to revive her career, she finds herself fending off his advances, and complicates matters even more when she tries to pass off Sam as her lover. As before, she leaves herself vulnerable to Sam— but he restrains himself as before.

Then begins her remarkable on-again, off-again romance with Robin Colcord, a romance which had even more twists and turns than the relationship between Sam and Diane, and in only half the time. All the while, a dim passion for Sam begins to develop, but Colcord's aura of money and power blinds her to this, as it does to his insincerity, cheating and his criminal activities. Even after he is jailed, she maintains her passion for him, only to endure a final humiliation at his hands. Eventually, she surprises everyone, including herself, by offering to bear Sam's child. How this will turn out has yet to be resolved— but it should be interesting, whatever happens.

Kirstie Alley faced an unenviable task, stepping into the vacancy left by Shelley Long to become Sam Malone's newest foil. She pulled it off admirably, making Rebecca Howe every bit as memorable a character as Diane Chambers. Of course, the two were apples and oranges from the outset. Whereas Diane was a supercilious intellectual with a suppressed passionate side, Rebecca was, and is, an ambitious go-getter who at first appeared to be made of ice. Thanks to Alley's superb comic acting, Rebecca soon developed her own depths, revealing a vulnerable side, as well as an endearing klutziness which often sabotages her attempts to further her career. As Sam's boss at the time of her debut, the dynamic tension between the two characters was of course quite the opposite of the Sam/Diane relationship, but Rebecca's tenure at Cheers has seen her endure some incredible reverses, including demotion to a cocktail waitress, an on-again, off-again with a British Donald Trump surrogate, Robin Colcord (Roger Rees), and the on-again, off-again realization that she really wants Sam (a realization she consistently backs away from). Perhaps the only predictable thing about Rebecca's relationship with Sam Malone is that it will be every bit as unpredictable as Sam's romance with Diane was during the first five years of *Cheers'* run.

In fact, the dark-haired, sultry-voiced Alley made her entrance onto the *Cheers* set dressed in Shelley Long drag: blonde wig, prim clothes. She even went so far as to have her eyebrows lightened with makeup. "I wanted to break the ice and get off to a fresh start," she claimed.

Any doubts she might have had about being accepted into the cast of the show were allayed when George Wendt (Norm) and John Ratzenberger (Cliff) gave her a shotgun, telling her that the only way she could ever get away from the show was to blast her way out past them!

Ted Danson concurred: "Stand us next to each other and it spells sex. I mean, sparks fly." Later, he added: "There will be comparisons made between Kirstie and Shelley, but in a while they'll all disappear."

These sentiments were echoed by Woody Harrelson, who portrays *Cheers'* slow but charming Woody Boyd: "She's hot, no doubt about it. She's got an interesting sexuality. She's got this quirky side, which I think is much more interesting."

Ironically, Kirstie Alley herself wasn't so sure about this sex appeal business. Of herself, she once observed, "I see someone with a crooked nose, my right eye's bigger than my left and sometimes I have zits. I also have this tiny face and lots of hair, which makes me look like Mrs. Potato Head."

Mrs. Potato Head? Kirstie Alley's not too likely to get anyone to agree with this vegetable assessment of herself, that's for sure. And at times, she's all too willing to let aside any thoughts of being a spud, such as when, one day on the *Cheers* set, she asked John Ratzenberger, "Am I TV's newest sex goddess?"

Ratzenberger's response was quick, and, under the circumstances, appropriate. "You're the *only* one!"

But then, the role of Rebecca Howe was tailored especially *for* Kirstie Alley. "They designed the role around me, with the same kind of quirks. Becky likes to see herself as very powerful. But she's kind of on the outs with the corporation she works for. This is her last chance. So one part of her is competent, brave, and successful, while the other side is totally neurotic. I wanted her to be very neurotic about physical things, about her body. A lot of women have serious hangups about their bodies."

And not just about looking like Mrs. Potato head, either. More realistically, she explains, "I get hangups about silly things. Like, do I have a mustache or do I not? Or if I get something on my face, is it skin cancer? It's always something dramatic. Not so much, ' are my thighs big?' but goofy things. Are my fingers too wrinkly looking? Are my knuckles too big? I get obsessed with little things."

Kirstey alley was born in Kansas. "[My father]," she recalls, "loved to play poker three or four times a week. He likes very basic things. And I was always different than that. I always wanted fast cars, horses, land. I should have been on *Dynasty*!"

"I always knew I wanted to act. I remember carrying around a picture of Linda Darnell when I was three years old, and I knew that was what I wanted to be."

24

But her path to acting and fame was almost derailed permanently. A dropout (after two years) of Kansas State University, Kirstie Alley's career may have been held back a bit by a two-year flirtation with cocaine. "I avoided drugs all during high school and college. Then someone said I'd really like cocaine. [I began] getting loaded on Fridays and Saturdays. It wasn't like I got up at six and hit it all day long," she points out, but the drug did seem to be in charge of her life for a while. "Like when my sister came over with her kids and I was loaded."

She gave up the habit on her own when its affect on her personal life became apparent. "I was whacked-out of my mind for two years. It wasn't good, but it wasn't a story of someone lying in the gutter. It was a personal failure.

"It caused a lot of damage. When I stopped doing drugs— cold turkey— I realized I'd affected other people's lives, so I wrote letters apologizing. I was a pretty unsettled person."

Now that she's clean and back to business, she drinks a particularly viscous (and possibly vicious) health drink. "It's Chinese herb tea. Ted recommended it. I just felt like I've abused my body enough. For thirty years its been body abuse in one way or another. Now I drink swamp water. It can't hurt. . . it cleans you out."

Once the drug problem was resolved, Kirstie Alley left Wichita, moved to Los Angeles and took a shot at acting. Before long, she landed roles in such television movies as *A Bunny's Story*, in which she portrayed Gloria Steinem in the true tale of Steinem's undercover investigation of working conditions at the Playboy Club, and *North and South* (both books), wherein she played a dedicated abolitionist during the War Between the States. In the movies, she created the role of Lieutenant Saavik in *Star Trek II: The Wrath of Khan,* and had roles in *Shoot To Kill* (with Tom Berenger) and *Loverboy* (with Patrick Dempsey). She almost got the Kathleen Turner role in *Body Heat*— a film which did feature future *Cheers* star Ted Danson. She also took some time to do theater as well, and played Maggie in a production of *Cat On A Hot Tin Roof*. One night, the audience included *Taxi* producer James Burrows, who remembered Alley four years later while seeking someone to fill the void left in the *Cheers* ensemble by the departure of Shelley Long. Alley was surprised: she had never done any comedic acting in her life. But she took the role, and the rest is television history: she's been a regular on *Cheers* every bit as long a time as her predecessor, and the show has maintained its popularity all throughout the Alley era.

In her personal life, Kirstie Alley is married to actor Parker Stevenson (once a Hardy Boy) and lives in Encino, California in a house once owned by Don Ameche— whose signature can be found, half-hidden, on part the building's wallpaper. Fans with outdated maps-of-the-stars'-homes sometimes intrude into Alley's domestic bliss, looking for the man who once played Alexander Graham Bell.

Alley, of course, has her own thoughts regarding marriage. "My parents were married for thirty-five years and loved each other madly, but they had a certain lifestyle. They ate dinner, then they ate Snickers and drank Cokes and watched TV, and they loved each other. And I thought that was the secret to marriage. Parker and I never lived together before we were married. So when I first got married I thought, 'This is the shock of my life!' Because we were so different. And I thought, 'This isn't what marriage is. This is *weird*.' And now it's more than I had imagined it would be. Now I love it."

But one very minor dispute fails to disrupt her happy marriage. It seems that when Alley and Stevenson spotted each a restaurant one night, they were both intrigued, and each wanted to meet the other. To this day, no one can determine which of the couple manipulated events (with the help of mutual friends such as Mimi Rogers, now married to Tom Cruise) so that they would meet. They were married in 1983, after Stevenson proposed, via letter, over dinner at L.A.'s exclusive L'Orangerie restaurant— he had the maitre d' deliver the letter over dinner.

Tragically, Alley's mother died in an automobile accident the same week that Alley landed her first major film role (Lieutenant Saavik in *Star Trek II: The Wrath of Khan*) and never saw her daughter's meteoric rise to stardom on both the large and small screens. "I think my family is really happy I'm now doing something I like," Alley observes, regretting her mother's absence. "She was a real character. She was real funny, because she thought meat needed to be cooked well-done. And her pork chops were always bowed. And I'd bring boyfriends over and would be embarrassed because the pork chops looked like leather!"

Since rising to prominence on *Cheers*, Kirstie Alley has continued to work in major motion pictures as well, including *Sibling Rivalry*, *Shoot To Kill* with Tom Berenger and Sidney Poitier, and with John Travolta in the wildly popular *Look Who's Talking* and its follow-up sequel, *Look Who's Talking, Too*.

Kirstie Alley and her husband share their home (originally built for Al Jolson. who moved into it a second time after Don Ameche vacated the premises) with an impressive menagerie of at least forty animals: cats, dogs, parrots, rabbits, mice and a horse comprise only part of the wild assortment. There are no children in the marriage yet, but Alley jokes about her art collection: "I have this vision of amassing art so my children can fight over it after I die." She chose the 22-room ranch style mansion in Encino because it reminded her of her home in Kansas in one essential.

"I thought the only way I could live in Los Angeles— I guess because I'm from Kansas and I'm used to land and space— is if we found a place that's flat. It had to be flat. I mean, I'm just not used to hills. So we came through those gates, and I thought, 'My God, a flat piece of land!'"

Another consideration was the ornamental pond filled with Japanese ornamental carp, or *koi*. The seller was going to sell them to someone else, but Alley was smitten by the beautiful fish, and insisted that they stay. Thus was the genesis of her now-impressive collection of pets, which also includes geese and cockatoos.

Her marriage with Parker Stevenson is strong, and she reasons that this is because they're both in the same business. "[Actors]. . . are the only people who understand why you're gone until two o'clock in the morning and why you have to get up again at four, and when you're shooting out of town and you're crazy and you come in and you've worked too much. . . they totally understand. You don't have to explain anything. If I was married to a librarian, I don't think he'd understand.

"I think three months is too long to be gone from each other. That's pushing it. So we go back and forth to each other's locations and make the effort to be with each other."

Of course, in addition to her continuing Cheers work, Kirstie Alley continues to work in motion pictures as well. ". . .I've gone back and forth between films and TV. I think Shelley [Long] is doing movies because she's a good actress. I don't think it's because she did TV or didn't do TV. I think good actors can do anything they want to do. When you hear actors say, 'You know, I just can't make that change over into film,' they can't act. They weren't that great on TV!"

WOODY HARRELSON (WOODY BOYD)

Not many people would have chosen Coach as their personal guru, but Midwesterner Woody Boyd, Coach's longtime pen-pal, apparently did, only to arrive in Boston too late to meet his hero. With nowhere to go, he became a fixture at the bar when Sam took pity on him. Woody's affable nature somehow overcomes his slow and peculiar take on life; simply put, everyone likes Woody. When he began to pine for his hometown gal Beth, the Cheers gang all chipped in to bring her to Boston for a reunion to soothe Woody's anxiety. When, soon afterward, Beth gets engaged to Woody's old rival, Woody pulls a stunt that only he can manage: of all the names in Sam's address book, woody manages to call Sam's cleaning woman— *and* hits it off with her!

Ever seeking self-improvement, Woody has also managed to develop a second career as an actor (bartending always coming first, of course). From bit parts and understudying, he has achieved such heights as a commercial representative for a vegetable drink, and as an extra on Robert Urich's *Spenser: For Hire* series. But his biggest success to date has been winning the heart of Kelly Gaines, the very innocent (and even more wealthy) daughter of a very wealthy man. Perhaps it is their mutual innocence and honest that has cut between their social differences, but this does not, of course, mean that their romance has not had its pitfalls. First there was her obnoxious boyfriend, followed by her mother, who seemed determined to woo Woody herself. Finally, her father has tried to come between her and Woody, but they have determined to be together someday— although Kelly's sojourn in Europe has produced a lecherous French teacher who seems determined to make Kelly his and his alone. But the Woodman will undoubtedly see things work out his way in the end. After all, few other characters on television can boast of having a pure heart (not that Woody would boast, if he were even aware of his own simplicity).

Woody Harrelson's name is just a coincidence. The slowly pensive Woody Boyd was created on paper before it was cast. After all this time, it seems fitting that the role should have gone to Woody Harrelson, who has slowly added layers of depth (admittedly, not too many layers) to the part he's played ever since Nicholas Colosanto (Coach) passed away. (Woody is not a nickname, but a shortened form of his given name, Woodrow.) As a naive

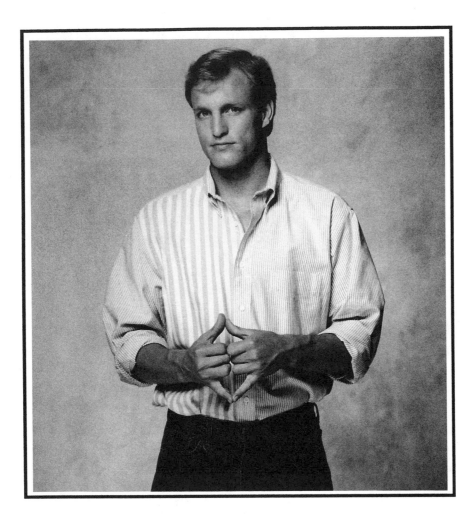

young man coming to the big, bean-cookin' city of Boston, Massachusetts with no goal other than to learn the mysteries of bartending with Coach as his guru, Woody (Harrelson, that is) slipped right into the swing of the *Cheers* ensemble.

In interviews, it's easy to tell the two Woodys apart. Harrelson drops the occasional multisyllabic word into his conversations and interviews. (It comes as a bit of a shock to first see such words as "dichotomy" and "parallel" attributed to him, it's true. . .) A fondness for the writings of Faulkner and Nabokov adds to the distance between them. But Woody H. likes Woody B., and brings his own innate intelligence to bear in making his television alter ego a real, likeable human being. This comes out best, perhaps, in Woody Boyd's ongoing relationship with the rich and beautiful Kelly Gaines, which frequently calls upon Woody Boyd to reveal his homespun Midwestern sense of personal dignity when faced with such snooty types as Kelly's arrogant boyfriend, flirtatious mother and overprotective father. The TV Woody has no asset other than himself, a trait perhaps shared by the real-life Woody, who was abandoned by his father at the age of seven.

Thirteen years later, Charles V. Harrelson came out of the woodwork in a most surprising fashion: he was tried and convicted as the hired killer of a Federal judge in San Antonio, Texas. (Ironically, the drug dealer who was charged with hiring Charles Harrelson as a hitman was not convicted.) Woody visits his father annually in the prison where he is serving his life sentence, and strives to develop a friendship with the man despite their years of estrangement. That Woody's childhood was marked by the absence of his father is indisputable; he was a classic troubled youth, prone to anger, until he accidentally discovered acting and learned to channel his energies that way. During college , he acted on stage extensively, and has since appeared in such strenuous plays as Tennessee Williams' *Cat On A Hot Tin Roof* and Edward Albee's *Zoo Story*. It's a sure bet that his Cheers fans wouldn't see much trace of Woody Boyd in such heavy dramas. More recently, he appeared on stage in Los Angeles in the new play *Brooklyn Laundry* with Glenn Close and Laura Dern, directed by James L. Brooks (*Terms of Endearment*). To top all this off, Harrelson has penned two plays of his own (*Two On Two* and *Furthest From The Sun*) and has recently toured with his own rock-and-roll band, Manly Moondog and The Three Kool Kats, a ten-member good-time musical ensemble. Harrelson is a triple threat within this context: he sings, plays guitar, and keyboards as well. (The band includes songwriter/guitarist Alfons Kettner and backup singer/Kool Kat Donny Gerrard. Says Harrelson, "We play R&B, rockabilly and rock'n'roll— sort of a mish-mash of those styles. We try and keep an open format."

Ironically, Hollywood's latest musical sensation doesn't much care for the L.A. scene: "I'd much rather play music out of this town. There's a different energy outside L.A. It seems to me, with the air here as bas as it is, people wouldn't be here in this city unless they were here for a reason. That reason creates a certain energy that I'd like to avoid. There's such a competitive thing here— such a focus on the need to succeed. It's hard to embrace these people [in L.A.]."

A performance in Fort Lauderdale elicited this response from Harrelson: "When it works like it did yesterday [in Fort Lauderdale], every atom in my body feels re-energized. It was a great audience. Hopefully, it will be the same situation [at the next performance]." Positive audience response seems to be undermining his previous uncertainties regarding his musical career move: "An actor trying to sing or do music is generally not an acceptable thing. So to a degree I understand people's 'prove it' attitude. But if I have to prove as I do, I'd rather it be more of an open-armed situation, away from L.A."

Concerned with environmental issues, much like his co-star Ted Danson, Harrelson recently took a strong stance in opposition to the Gulf War, a move which lost him gigs as the Grand Marshall for the Mardi Gras this past year in New Orleans, and as a spokesperson for Miller Beer. But Harrelson stands by his beliefs and takes these minor setbacks in stride. He also puts a certain amount— but not too much— of his views into his music. "I realize there are people out there who say 'enough with this message stuff, we want to hear music.' But I say its okay to mix a little heavy with the lightness. I think we have come up with a healthy mix."

"We are having an awful lot of fun with this," he is quick to add. "I just love to connect with people. I've been very gregarious and outgoing since I was very young. I just love getting up and performing. I exist to do this band right now."

He started playing music early, in fact: "I used to have this little snare drum, and my older brother John would be lead vocalist— he was the older brother— and we'd sit and play along with the Beatles albums, and I'd sing backup. We used to love it. Then we started charging a nickel entry fee, and we lost our audience."

In a way, Harrelson prefers live performance— musical or theatrical— to television or film. "I need an immediate response," he observes. "You've got a character to hid behind, in a way," he notes of stage acting. "It's not you out there, vulnerable-izing yourself. Not sure if that's a word, but when I make myself vulnerable on stage musically it's really a frightening thing— and the payoff can be really phenomenal!"

But Woody Harrelson's film career is now beginning to stir, as well; his first lead role will be against Wesley Snipes in the basketball movie *White Men Can't Jump*, directed by *Bull Durham* director Ron Shelton. His supporting role in the Michael J. Fox comedy *Doc Hollywood* gave him the last word in that film, a volley in his good-natured "feud" with one of his *Cheers* costars. When, in that film's final scene, someone points out an offscreen individual that they think is a famous movie star, Harrelson's character retorts, "No, that's just Ted Danson." With a healthy, irreverent attitude like that, Woody Harrelson is bound to go far.

RHEA PERLMAN (CARLA TORTELLI)

O f all the regulars at Cheers, barmaid Carla undoubtedly has the most convoluted personal history of anyone there. Divorced from the sleazy Nick Tortelli (Dan Hedaya), she soon finds herself pregnant by another man, and considering snaring someone else to give her baby a father, even though she reconsiders when the gentleman in question agrees to marry her even though he isn't even the father. When her ex-husband Nick shows up, she almost gives him custody of their son Anthony; even though he's a sleazeball, she's still sort of crazy about Nick. But cooler heads prevail, and Carla stands up to her ex.

Between rounds in her varied familial conflicts, Carla took great delight in tormenting Diane Chambers, especially by forcing her to face the truth of Sam Malone's lustful attentions to other women. When Diane left, Carla was (temporarily, at least) without a foil, although she must have been relieved that Sam wasn't getting married to Diane after all; Carla carries a secret torch for Sammy.

After a brief reunion with the still-despicable Nick— strictly for the purpose of winning a dance contest, however— Carla met Eddie LeBec, a hockey goalie on a hot winning streak. Unfortunately, Carla seemed to be a jinx for Eddie, who started to lose as soon as they got together. An on-again, off-again arrangement (there have always been a lot of those on *Cheers*) solves this problem, but when Carla and Eddie finally get married, Eddie is fired. To complicate matters further, Carla's son Anthony and his young bride moved in with them, too, leaving her to support an entire family by serving drinks to the lowlifes at Cheers.

Eddie's new career as a skating penguin in an ice show was short lived, as was Eddie himself; a Zamboni ice machine cut him down in the prime of life, leaving Carla to face his death— and the fact that he was a bigamist, leaving a second widow behind. Never one to leave well enough alone, Carla becomes convinced that Eddie is haunting her, but luckily a fraudulent medium puts the spirit, and Carla's nerves, to rest, leaving her to carry on with her life.

Snarling at customers and co-workers alike, ready to fight, with awful and vicious vengeance, every slight, real or imagined, and mothering, at last count, eight children, Carla LeBec (formerly Tortelli, née Lozupone) might seem an unlikely candidate for one of television's most popular characters. . . but she

is just that, a heroine to those of us who have taken just about enough nonsense in our lives but can't quite work up the petty vindictiveness necessary to cope with the angst and the frustration. A far cry from the soft-spoken Rhea Perlman, who first appeared on television with any regularity as Louie DePalma's girlfriend Zena Sherman on the Burrows/Charles/Charles series *Taxi*. She is also married to the man behind Louie, Danny DeVito (they lived together for eleven years before marrying), who she met when they were both struggling actors in the dog-eat-dog of the New York theatre world. She first saw DeVito in an off-Broadway production. "[Danny] had an insane part, a really dumb part, but he dominated the whole stage, all that energy. He had a handle on the part and I felt he also had a handle on life." Perlman's strangest employment during this period was a job erasing pencil marks out of used books.

When DeVito headed to the West Coast to direct a project for the American Film Institute, a dubious Perlman followed him there, picking up TV-movie roles, then the occasional part on *Taxi*, finally culminating in her casting as Carla on *Cheers*. Some have noted that the role is, to all effects, a female Louie DePalma, but no one will deny that Rhea Perlman has made the part her own. *Cheers* also provides work for other members of the Perlman family: Heidi

Perlman, Rhea's sister, is a writer as well as story editor for the series, and her father Phil Perlman, a former doll manufacturer, has appeared as an extra in the background of the bar on numerous occasions.

"He's an extra, and he's sixty-seven years old and a little balding, but kind of dapper. And I really like him because. . . he's my father. He's having a ball [doing *Cheers*]. Maybe he'll have a line someday, and it will be great fun.

Now he's going to work on other shows, too, and he's like a little kid. You know, it's a little like having your dad come to school!"

Phil Perlman observes the key differences between his daughter and the role she portrays. "I try to look at Rhea as just a character when we're working on the show. Some of the things they give her to say— well, Carla's a tough lady, and it just rolls off me. Now Rhea. . . [she] happens to be a very sweet, lovely little lady."

Rhea Perlman married Danny DeVito after eleven years of living together. When they married, the theme music was a record of "I'm In The Mood For Love"— sung by Alfalfa, of *Our Gang* fame. The ceremony was performed by a minister friend, Ralph Pyle, whose main occupation is that of French horn player for the Los Angeles Philharmonic. Married life agrees with the couple; Perlman comments on their professional interactions:

"We certainly talk to each other about problems in our scripts, and try to help. Sometimes, I ask him to watch something and tell me what he thinks of it, and I do the same for him. That's one of the most fun parts in our relationship. But there's been nothing formal. I think that living with him— he is such a good actor— rubs off on you. If you're lucky, it rubs off. In that way, he helps me a lot. But he never gives me advice. Doing a character is a kind of delicate thing. You can't have somebody not involved in the show do a whole lot in helping with the characterization."

Perlman recalls her Jewish family when she was a child: "We were the kind of people who pulled down the shades on Yom Kippur, you know, when you're supposed to fast, and we ate, ate, ate. You're not supposed to drive either, so we parked the car around the corner, then got in."

"Mom is a bookkeeper and Dad manages a doll parts store. You go in and see all those little eyes and arms."

In her youth, Perlman wanted to be an actress, but "I was too shy to talk in public, she admits. "[And] for years I used to say I was an actress and I said it so apologetically that people did'nt seem to believe me. Maybe I didn't even believe it myself. But now I can look the whole world in the eye and say 'Hey, I'm an actress.' And I sound convincing."

Perlman admits her biggest secret easily: "I might as well tell you. I'm not Carla. I never came up with a snappy line in my life."

Shelley Long seconded this motion: "Rhea is about as far from Carla as she could possibly be. She's quiet, shy and doesn't have any of Carla's angst."

"Rhea deeply cares about what she's doing, whether it's her family or her work. She's a very conscientious lady. I've compared her, as an actress, to Thelma Ritter, who was always one of my favorites. She has that wonderful, disarming quality of candid, blunt comedy."

Perlman and DeVito live with their children, Lucy and Gracie, in Hollywood, nearby the Griffith Observatory. "When I was up for Cheers, I knew it was the most critical moment of my life and I said, 'If I don't get it, I'm going to have a baby. Then I said, "If I do get it, I'm going to have a baby."

"When I was younger I used to hate the whole kid scene, birthday parties, all the bags the mothers carried, the diapers. And Danny [Devito] and I had never been tied down. Just before Lucy (their first child) came we were both kind of scared. We knew we would be caring parents. . . but would we enjoy it? Well, it's been more fun than either of us dreamed."

When Shelley Long left *Cheers*, Rhea Perlman contemplated the effect that this might have on her character. "I mean, I could break down the wall of my dressing room, and then I could have a bedroom and a living room, since Shelley's dressing room is right next door to me. That could be a benefit. It's got a window in it.

Obviously, there's going to be a big vacancy in the tone of the show. It won't be about Sam and Diane any more, which is really the basis of *Cheers*. I don't know what it is going to be about, which is kind of exciting after you've been with something for five years. A change could be fun."

And of course, *Cheers* carried on to new heights with the arrival of Kirstie Alley as Rebecca Howe. Once again, Carla had a nemesis, and a focus for her hostility. There seems to be no end in sight— Carla still rules Cheers with an iron fist, even if nobody else quite realizes it!

GEORGE WENDT (NORM PETERSON)

If Carla's personal life has covered the most ground in the course of the ten-year run of Cheers, then Norm Peterson's employment has been the most varied. When we first met him, he was employed as an accountant in the firm of H.W. Sawyer; he attempted to get in his boss' good graces by throwing a toga party— but poor old hapless Norm was the only one to show up in a toga! To make matters worse, Norm feels obliged to defend Diane's honor when Sawyer hits on her, and he winds up butting heads with his own employer.

Norm's never-seen wife Vera, apparently the primary reason for his long hours at the bar, is the one constant in his life. He once left her but soon encountered his old high school rival Wally Bodell, who seemed to feel that Norm's withdrawal has left Vera fair game. This got Norm's dander up, reawakening his love for Vera. Norm and Wally end up settling, right in the middle of the bar, an old high-school wrestling rivalry; not a pretty sight, watching two large men flop around on the floor like battling whales.

Norm's freelance accountancy has led to its own complications as well, such as the time that Norm erroneously deduced that the IRS owed Sam thirty thousand dollars in tax refunds. Temptation also arose when a client, Emily, took a fancy to Mr. Peterson— but he was faithful to Mrs. Peterson once again.

Once, thinking himself doomed (by way of the old mixed-up X-ray routine), Norm goes off to wander the world during his last days— only to be discovered living in the stockroom at the back of the bar!

An agreement to cover Cliff's mail route lands Norm in jail at one point in this wide-ranging career; another boss discovers Norm at the bar and threatens to fire him unless Norm becomes his hatchet man— a job Norm is spectacularly unsuited for.

In one embarrassing turn of events, Norm had an affair with a neighbor's wife in retaliation for the neighbor's apparent affair with Vera— only to discover that Vera has been faithful all along. fortunately, nothing much comes of this, although Norm is considerably chastened.

Ever on the lookout for new business, Norm invests, disastrously, in a combination laundromat/tanning salon. Fortunately, he is more successful as a housepainter, which in turn leads to a career as an interior decorator— al-

though Norm is afraid that he must act 'gay' if he is to properly impress his yuppie clients. Fortunately, as always, Norm discovers that he can succeed and be himself as well. . . and his quest for the right career goes on. Of course, his true calling is drinking beer— and trading quips with Cliff Clavin.

Enter Norm. "My shorts are riding up."

Cliff inquires: "Why don't you stand up and straighten them out?"

Norm is nonplussed by this inquiry. "Nah, I'll give them five minutes. Sometimes they self-adjust."

In a similar vein, Norm once observed: "It's a dog-eat-dog world— and I'm wearing milkbone underwear."

George Wendt, the actor behind Norm Peterson, throws off some of *Cheers'* best lines, filling out a role that was originally intended as nothing more than the archetypal fellow who stops into a bar for just one beer and ends up staying the entire night. Norm— the real hero of the show? Maybe. His arrival invariably signals the beginning of any given episode's action, and he and his mailman pal Cliff Clavin (John Ratzenberger), when not featured in the main body of the plot, always serve as the show's modern redefinition of the classical Greek chorus. They comment wryly on the inescapable comic turmoil before and around them.

George Wendt's grandfather was a newspaperman, "a superstar of yellow journalism; the equipment he used to take the famous hidden-camera photograph of the execution of Ruth Snyder is in the Smithsonian."

Born and raised in Chicago (home of. . .yes. . . "da Bullz"), Wendt attended a strict Jesuit prep school, and then dropped out of Notre Dame University after a few uneventful years. (Regarding his early, Jesuit education, he observes that Notre Dame, by comparison, seemed "like Sodom and Gomorrah.") He admits that he was "not motivated to do anything but have fun." His dropping out was largely inspired by the fact that he forgot to take his finals one semester (he must have really been having fun), which resulted in an amazing 0.0 grade point average. He graduated from a different, less prestigious college.

After spending these seemingly fruitless years getting educated, Wendt then wandered aimlessly around Europe for a few more. Remembers Wendt: "Those times were so relaxing, I can't believe it now. The big three occupations were doing your laundry, brushing your teeth and writing post cards. Laundry was always a spotty proposition, you were lucky if you brushed your teeth, and if you wrote a post card, you really accomplished something that day."

Eventually, Wendt wound up returning to his home town and going out for what appeared to be the most painless job around— working with the Windy City's famed Second City comedy troupe. "This was it for running away. I'd had enough. I'd used the process of elimination; I went down as many occupations as I could think of— teacher, doctor, accountant— trying to figure out, 'What don't I hate?' I'd gone to Second City in Chicago a lot during my college days. I thought, 'Boy, that looks like I wouldn't hate it. And I'm pretty sure they get paid.' It was the first time I had any inkling of being determined to do anything in life."

From 1974 to 1980, Wendt enjoyed an on-again, off-again relationship with the improvisational group. His low point during this period came one night when he was actually booed off the stage ("Really mortifying, the low point of my career"), but he persevered, honing his acting talents in the process. A failed television pilot, "Nothing But Comedy," brought him and his family to Los Angeles, where he was anything but an overnight success.

"I was so wired after the high-pressure, gung-ho atmosphere of Second City that doing two days on a sitcom and that's it for six months was traumatic. I went kind of crazy. I holed up in the house for months like a hermit, sitting around in my gym shorts watching TV. {Bernadette] kind of snapped me out of it. I was turning into just a lump."

But things took a turn for the better when a bit part as an exterminator on *Taxi* brought Wendt to the attention of James Burrows and the Charles brothers, who remembered him when they were casting *Cheers*. So certain were they that he was right for the role that they gave it to him even though he was involved in another comedy show, *Making The Grade*, which died an early but merciful death which left Wendt free to concentrate on *Cheers*.

Wendt is married to actress Bernadette Birkett, who occasionally provides the off-screen voice of Norm's eternally unseen wife Vera; the couple, who have two sons and a daughter, met while working at the Second City.

In addition to his ongoing Cheers work, Wendt has appeared in a number of films, including *Thief of Hearts, Fletch* (with Chevy Chase), *House, No Small Affair,* and *Dreamscape.* Of his super-slob role in Fletch, Wendt commented: "I didn't have to worry about spilling ketchup on my shirt during lunch. . . the grubbier, the better."

Wendt has also hosted *Saturday Night Live,* where he created the role of a Chicago sports fan whose cronies can think of no topics of discussion beyond the Bears and the Bulls (with occasional considerations of Chicago's other, less prominent sports franchises). Wendt has also returned, unannounced, to take part in further sketches involving these characters, and joined the rest of the *Cheers* cast in surprising Kirstie Alley when she hosted *Saturday Night Live* early in its 1991 season. His most recent big screen appearance was a dramatic role with Robert DeNiro in Irwin Winkler's *Guilty By Suspicion.*

John Ratzenberger has described George Wendt thus: "He has great throwaway delivery. Some guys throw away lines; he throws away his whole performance. [George] makes good comedy look so effortless. He just knows what's right. Even on the first day we read a script, he'll wander over and whisper about certain lines. 'That'll be cut,' and sure enough, it's gone the next day. Whatever he has, he didn't have to learn it anywhere. He was born with it."

Ted Danson also finds Wendt's presence and skill invaluable. "When we're rehearsing, part of me has got my eye on George to check myself out as we're working. He's really good at letting me know when I'm going too far or not far enough."

Wendt himse;f states that, "I'm not that good an actor. My life is nothing like Norm's. [Norm] is a little dumber, a little cruder, a little slimier, a bit more spineless," than the real George Wendt. How much less? He's not about to reveal that much. He does admit, however, to being decidedly un-hip, especially in Hollywood. "I sort of feel out of it in terms of haircuts and clothes. I'm more of a Valley kind of guy; I like a little bit of Peoria." Of his fondness for lounging in swimming pools, he quips, "I must have been a manatee in my former life."

Ratzenberger's awe at Wendt's skills is not limited to his acting, however. "He's a legendary barbecue chef. Everyone else will be partying and he's sitting next to his Weber, his ear up against it, not moving for three hours, listening to the damn thing cook. all of a sudden he'll get up and pour and ounce of beer in there real fast. 'They tell me when they're done,' he claims."

In a similar vein is Rhea Perlman's terse but accurate comment about the large Wendt: "He does *not* avoid food."

Wendt is also hungry for information, and reads at least four newspapers a day. "USA Today would have been the deal breaker," he reacalls. "My wife said, 'One more newspaper and the marriage is kaput!'"

All this reading leads into another facet of George Wendt, again saluted by John Ratzenberger: "[George is like] Paul Bunyan with the soul of Bertrand Russell, a very easygoing guy with a finely honed intelligence, which I didn't realize until he whipped my keister in Trivial Pursuit."

Norm beating Cliff at Trivial Pursuit? This, truly, is an amazing difference between fiction and reality.

The 235-pound Wendt's attitude toward his size is no-nonsense. "I wish I were thinner, and I certainly don't want to get any fatter. {But] I have it lucky. I don't have to worry about losing hair, crows' feet, or putting on weight." The only problem is going out in public: "I cut a mean profile. Shades won't hide that, my figure makes it hard to escape detection."

Of course, Norm specializes in getting the final word in, as exemplified by the following exchange:

Cliff: "In all the years you've known me, why didn't you ever tell me I was a blowhard?"

Norm: "I kept trying to squeeze it in."

Cliff: "Thanks, Norm. I know that must have been hard to say—"

Norm: "You're ugly, too."

As far as *Cheers* and Norm Petersen are concerned, George Wendt is one happy fellow. "I can't worry to much about the future. This is now, and in the opinion of a lot of folks, *Cheers* is the coolest comedy on TV. It may be a depressing thought, but I may never again wind up with a role as cool as Norm. This is it. It doesn't get any better."

CHEERS

JOHN RATZENBERGER (CLIFF CLAVIN)

Sometimes it seems that Cliff Clavin knows *everything*. Everything in the realm of the useless, that is. "The Bermuda Triangle is actually a trapezoidal rhomboid. . ." Thanks, Cliff. But what does that actually mean*?!?*

But there's more (or perhaps less) to Cliff Clavin than meets the eye. Everyone thought he was a coward when he avoided confronting a man who was threatening him; Cliff maintained that he just didn't want to hurt the *guy*. And he may have been right. But there *is* a certain level of cowardice to Cliff. Not an endearing trait. Certainly not the time he refused to step forward (at least at first) when Norm, who had graciously agreed to cover Cliff's mail route, was arrested for impersonating a postal carrier. Or is he truly a noble fellow, as the time he took the rap for his girlfriend Margaret when they misappropriated a postal vehicle for an illicit motel tryst? Hard to say.

If Cliff has a weakness, it is women. He just doesn't know how to cope with them. When Margaret tried to rope him into marriage, he developed all kinds of psychosomatic illness that seemed almost to cripple him. When he planned to sue the owner of a dog that bit him, he was easily suckered into relinquishing all claims by the voluptuous woman in question. Face it: where women are involved, Cliff is a sap and a sucker. He can't even break away from his mother. But sit Cliff down in a barstool next to Norm Peterson, give him a stein of beer, and he'll never want for something to say— even if it's sometimes hard to figure out what, if anything, his comments have to do with the world around him.

John Ratzenberger brings Cliff Calvin to life. It may come as no surprise that a great many of the mailman's tangential, obscure observations are ad-libbed. Ratzenberger subscribes to a variety of intriguing but little known technical magazines, and has a strong background in improvisation. Glen Charles, co-executive producer of *Cheers*, confirms this:

"He's an improviser. In terms of Cliff spewing trivia, we typically supply just the start of it in the script, then John takes it off into orbit."

In fact, John Ratzenberger practically created the role of Cliff for himself. He was originally considered for the role of Norm, but realizing that he hadn't

42

wowed the producers much, he took a long shot and pitched them the idea of a know-it-all character for the bar— an indispensable part of reality that James Burrows and the Charles brothers had somehow managed to overlook in their original concept for the show. "I'm walking out the door and I know I've failed Norm. Not failed exactly, but you know whether you've done something that's got the producers excited or not. So I thought, 'Give it a shot, John, you're exiting anyway.' I turned around and said, 'Listen, do you have a bar know-it-all?' They said no. I said, 'Every bar has one,' and went into a ten-minute dissertation on this guy, picking up things in the office for props. They started laughing and kept laughing."

The occasional role of Cliff soon became a mainstay of the series, and Cliff's barstool, right next to Norm's, is one of the most hallowed spots on the *Cheers* set.

Born in Bridgeport, Connecticut, of Hungarian ancestry, John Ratzenberger attended Catholic school, where he encountered strong influences on his later life. He recalls that some "Irish kids I hung around with, Jim Shannon and Tom Connery, [were] the funniest people I've ever met, to this day.

He attributes his sense of timing to "Sister Regina at my Catholic grammar school. A hawkeye. When I was able to make Shannon and Connery break up any number of times without getting caught myself by Sister Regina, I knew I had a future in show business."

Ratzenberger's father "used to interrupt dinner, sailing through the kitchen doing a Jack E. Leonard impression, twirling his hat as he went out the door. Sometimes he even came back. At six o'clock on Sunday mornings, his one day off from driving a truck, he'd put a Louis Prima-Keely Smith album on the hi-fi, more than loud enough to roust all of us out of bed. Well, how could you have a real dour outlook when you're surrounded by characters, including your own father, from day one? I'd never trade it for growing up with the Colby's, that's for sure."

Ratzenberger went on to attend Sacred Heart University, where he teamed up with a classmate to create a two-man improvisational act, "Sal's Meat Market." The team toured Europe for the better part of half a decade, receiving a grant from Great Britain's Arts Council— a first for any American performers. Once the popular show folded, Ratzenberger made ends meet by doing some writing for the BBC and from earnings gleaned form parts in such European-filmed motion pictures as *A Bridge Too Far* and *Yanks*. Generally, his times in England were lean ones, culminating in his taking a job as a tree surgeon's assistant— a job poorly suited for the acrophobic Ratzberger. "The low point of my life," he later recollected. "A ketchup sandwich then was the big treat of the day. Plus, I hate heights. So it came down to a matter of either climbing up the stepladder and up that tree, or I didn't get paid and I didn't eat. I went up, but that's when I decided I'd better get serious about acting. . . acting that paid off!"

Ratzenberger decided to return to the United States and pursue acting in earnest. Once he pitched his encyclopedic barfly character to the producers of *Cheers*, there was no doubt that he was going to make it.

Ratzenberger couldn't help but observe differences between the United States and Europe after his decade-long sojourn abroad. "When I first came back to the States, I was struck by how much metal it took to make American cars. Nobody needs cars that big. If anything rules here, it's greed and an attitude of take, take, take without giving back. We've been taking so much for so long it's hard to know where you can go and safely drink tap water in the country. The environment is starting to pay us back. I'm not saying it's only an American problem, but at least Europeans are more adjusted to the limits."

Of his stay in Europe, Ratzenberger recounts: "I was face-to-face every day for a decade with the fact that Americans are held in high disregard in Europe. Part of the reason is that the television garbage we export makes Europeans think we're liars, cheats, robbers and people who sleep with our best friends' wives. They think we're represented by J.R."

Not inappropriately, Cliff Clavin is hailed nationwide by members of the postal profession, who have made John Ratzenberger an honorary member of their organization. "There are Cliffs everywhere," reflects Ratzenberger. "I don't know how many postal workers have told me they have one in their local branch."

"The most challenging thing I have to do with Cliff is to show him intimidated by women. I grew up with two sisters, one older, one younger, and I've always been comfortable around women. In fact, one of the reasons I stayed in England ten years is that I was a bachelor then and there's no Puritan ethic there. Remember, the Puritans left to come here."

Ratzenberger has also followed in the footsteps of George Wendt, by playing a neighbor in *House II.*

His popularity in his home town of Bridgeport, Connecticut is so great that he's been honored by the town. "I'm the grand marshall he the annual parade," he proudly recounts, "and as we start out [one year], my driver, a childhood buddy, cuts in front of the mayor's car—'Hey, Ratzie gos first!'

So I don't think the mayor was thrilled about that, but what really got him is when I started hollering things to the people lining the streets; 'Hey, there's no trees on this street. Tell the mayor you deserve some trees!' Then I'd look back and people would be yelling at the mayor. 'We're paying our taxes and we ain't got any trees! What kinda government ya runnin' here?' Then there'd be a street with all kinds of trees, so I'd holler for people to complain they can't get any sunshine. Here comes the mayor, grinning and waving, and all of a sudden he's being accosted because there are too damn many trees. By the time we got to the stand for the ceremonies, the poor guy was reeling!"

"That night I'm at a local gin mill with a lot of people I grew up with, and a woman comes over. Maureen. I've known Maureen forever. She says, 'Ratz, you've done so well for yourself, look at you. You go to London and now you're back and you're on national TV. We're all so proud of you.' Well, I'm really touched; I reach for the handkerchief, you know, to dab at the eyes and do some nose-snuffling. Then Maureen says, 'Yeah, Ratz, I can't figure it out— in school you were always so dumb!'"

George Wendt has a bit more respect for Ratzenberger: "John automatically bestows respect on anyone he meets, and he won't tolerate any lack of respect toward himself in return.'

Of course, it's difficult not to respect a man who has been known to use a water pistol on people who annoy him by talking in movie theaters.

Recalls Ratzenberger: "The Smithsonian Institution has this wonderful film about men in flight that makes you want to lose yourself in the beauty of it, but a couple in the theater kept chattering out loud, spoiling the whole thing. I stood up, turned around, and screamed at them at the top of my lungs. The rest of the audience gave me a big hand."

Popular on screen as well as off, its obvious that John Ratzenberger will always be a mainstay of the *Cheers* experience.

KELSEY GRAMMER (FRASIER CRANE)

Dr. Frasier Crane, psychiatrist, first appeared as yet another complication in the Sam Malone/Diane Chambers romance: he was the psychiatrist Diane turned to after her romance with an arrogant, pompous painter (Christopher Lloyd) fell apart. Contrary to professional ethics, Frasier became involved with his beautiful, intelligent patient— but it was destined to fail from the start.

At first, his affair a secret, Frasier tried to help Sam deal with his own rejection by Diane. . .not really a good move, but no worse than his next one, which was to turn to Sam for help when Diane persisted in calling Dr. Crane by Mr. Malone's name. This sloppy maneuver was at least redeemed by Diane, who pretended to get back with Sam just so she could call him 'Frasier' in the 'throes' of passion!

Classic Freudian themes came into play when Frasier's mother, herself a respected psychiatrist, came into town and pronounced that Diane could only ruin Frasier's career—even going so far as to threaten Ms. Chambers with death. Things looked brighter when she left town; Diane moved in with Frasier, only to discover that she was allergic' at first seemingly to Frasier's beloved dog, but perhaps, ultimately, to Frasier himself. Cohabitation was not a successful move. Frasier was even more bewildered when his psychiatric teacher and mentor fell head over heels in lust for Carla!

Ultimately, Frasier went to Europe to teach, taking Diane along. But their wedding plans were foiled when Diane left Frasier stranded at the altar in order to enter a convent instead.

In time Diane returned, but not to Frasier. Soon enough, Diane was gone for good; Frasier Crane stayed on. The desperate shrink almost marries the first girl Sam sets him up with, only to fall for the formidable Dr. Lilith Sternin (a staunch Jungian in contrast to his mainline Freudianism) when they are reunited for a televised psychiatric debate. Romance soon ensues between these two uptight brains; they are soon living together, and Lilith has no troublesome allergies to spoil their bliss. A proposal, a wedding and a baby boy all follow in due course.

Sine Lilith is Jewish, they decide to have a traditional bris, (circumcision ceremony) for their son, but a sort of castration anxiety assails Frasier, and he tries to 'save' his son from this fate, only to be reconciled in the end. It's smooth

sailing from this point on, except when Lilith's new pop psychology book tags Frasier as a boring, nice guy, and he runs off (briefly— very briefly) with a tattooed biker chick named Viper.

Kelsey Grammer originally signed on to portray psychiatrist Frasier Crane in a limited, seven-episode part. The character was simply a stuffed-shirt straw man to complicate the course of the romance between Sam Malone and Diane. Thanks to the nuances of dignity and wit brought to the role by Grammer, the character stayed on long after Diane Chambers became a fading memory. "He made an unlikable character likeable," is executive producer James Burrows' salute to Grammer.

Ted Danson also has kudos for the new shrink on the block. "He brings a breadth of experience to the role. Sometimes I wish they'd let him become an all-out degenerate so he could show his range!"

Kelsey Grammer entered the world on Saint Thomas island in the Virgin Islands, where his father, an unusual sort and a free spirit (much like Kelsey would someday become) ran a bar, gave musical instruction, and published a newspaper. When Kelsey was five years old, his parents broke up, and he soon found himself living with his grandparents in New Jersey. His grandfather, Grammer recalls, was "a liberal conservative, a situational philosopher. Dinner was always a time for conversation. After the dishes were cleared, my grandfather and I would talk over the day's events and what had been learned at school."

When Grammer was twelve, the family moved to Florida, where his grandfather died within the week. "I guess it had to do with his dying. I became a recluse, a loner. I went through the usual sort of peer ostracism. Originally, they ostracized me, and then, finally, I didn't really care about them very much. I was alone a good deal of the time. I liked to surf and then go home and meditate.'

Somehow, young Grammer wound up in a high school production of *The Little Foxes*.

"I was taking my bow after the first performance, and I thought, 'Now this I can do for the rest of my life and it would still be really like surfing.' It was exciting, engaging. And it has a kind of freedom. Surfing was my faith. It's like a functional realization of Zen philosophy. Acting is also moment to moment, if it's any good. You just go with the wave of a play and you ride it, and you don't necessarily conquer it. You spend time together."

As a student , Grammer eventually left the acting department at the Julliard School. "Well, they threw me out, really," he later reminisced. "We weren't getting along. They kept asking me if I really wanted to be an actor. I knew I did, but I didn't want to go on trying to prove it to them by their recognized formula."

Tragedy struck when his younger sister was murdered by a serial killer. "That was the worst part of my life. I had a huge hole open in terms of my emotional stability."

Grammer, the ex-surfer and piano player then kicked around through various odd jobs up and down the East Coast, from New York to Florida and back again. Chance landed him a role onstage at San Diego's Old Globe Theater, where he decided to return to acting as a serious commitment. "It was like completing college. I had a ball. [But] I had to defeat New York. I had felt a bit overwhelmed by it before." New York, marriage, a daughter and a divorce ensued in short order. "We're not together. . . after the wedding ceremony, it got rocky. It was like we had one great day, our wedding day, and then it started rocking.

"At one point [during the divorce proceedings] I was asked to give her more money than I had ever made in a year."

Grammer now lives with his girlfriend, skater Cerlette Lammé, in the San Fernando Valley, where he collects old cars, including an Oldsmobile, a Cadillac, and his personal favorite, a 1972 Triumph. He shares his home not only with Cerlette but with an indeterminate number of dogs. He spotted Cerlette in the audience one night while he was performing in a Los Angeles stage production of Shakespeare's *Measure For Measure*, and had a note hand-delivered to her by the theater's house manager. They've been together ever since. Grammer's friends call his oddly ramshackle home "Fort Grammer"; he certainly lives an unorthodox life, but that's okay by him.

In 1984, the role of Frasier Crane came up. Recalls Grammer: "I was asked to read for this new character. They were very secretive about it. No one could see the script. It was like industrial espionage. I had not even seen

48

the show at all, so I didn't even know what I was auditioning for. [But] I just knew I could do it." In fact, he objected when the Crane character began dating Diane Chambers, his patient. "Frasier Crane is a great psychiatrist! And that's unprofessional."

Making the move to television was awkward for the stage-trained Grammer. "I was very nervous. You know, doing television, when you're an 'actor.' I thought, 'Oh God, I'll get trapped. I'll never do anything again but play this character Frasier Crane."

Ironically, Kelsey Grammer's fame veered upwards in 1988 in the wake of his arrest for the possession of approximately twenty-five dollars worth of cocaine. Grammer was already facing new troubles in the wake of a 1987 drunk driving conviction: his failure to make a court date to present proof of his rehabilitation led to a revocation of his probation, and he got the maximum punishment for that offense. The aftermath of his drug arrest unfolded in much the same way, as Grammer twice failed to show up at scheduled court appearances; his troubles only eascalated thanks to this pattern of behavior. Part of the problem was his concern over his girlfriend Cerlette's illness, which included seizures, but the judge in his case, Aviva K. Bobb, declined to let Grammer slide on this account: "We all have other responsibilities," observed the judge, setting Grammer's bail bond at $7,500.

In fact, Cerlette was suffering from pressure on her sinuses, which affected her nerves; the situation was rectified by surgery. Grammer's attorney, Robert L. Diamond, has observed, "He was counting on his girlfriend; she normally would have reminded him [of his scheduled court appearances]. He leads a life where people continually tell him what to do the next day. When someone says, 'See you in February 1990,' he just can't keep that kind of calendar. . . They know he's a really talented guy. The only thing he isn't good at is appointments and dates."

Cerlette Lammé pointed out at the time, "He's been real worried about me. I know it's no excuse, but it's true." Eventually, with the help of drug rehabilitation and the moral support of his *Cheers* co-stars, Grammer cleaned up his act. In retrospect, he recalls that he ". . . really enjoyed doing drugs, but lost sight of where the fun was." In the aftermath of these experiences, however, Grammer continues his career unhindered, both as Frasier Crane on *Cheers* and as the voice of Sideshow Bob on the hit animated series *The Simpsons*.

BEBE NEUWIRTH (LILITH STERNIN-CRANE)

When originally hired for Cheers, Bebe Neuwirth was originally intended to be on just a couple episodes. But the writers kept coming up with more ideas for her character, particularly in the way she perfectly complimented Frasier Crane. Whereas Frasier seemed to be a loose wheel for awhile the way he kept turning up after Diane left him at the alter, once Lilith entered the picture, Fraser's character had an anchor which made him firmly a part of the show. One of the truly classic episodes occurred when Sam and Diane had gotten back together and visited Frasier and Lilith for dinner. In the course of conversation, it slipped out that Frasier had once cohabitated with Diane, a fact Frasier had never revealed to Lilith even though she knew that Diane had left Frasier standing at the alter in Italy. Arguments erupted first between Lilith and Frasier, and then between Sam and Diane and the women would take turns locking themselves in the bedroom until finally Sam and Frasier locked both Lilith and Diane in the bedroom together so they could have dinner in peace.

Dr. Lilith Sternin, Jungian shrink and totally in self-control, joined the ranks of the *Cheers* cast when she debated Frasier Crane on a television show. Crane was petrified by her, only to find himself attracted to her when the debate took on sexual undercurrents. Lilith's dour, deadpan delivery belies an underlying tension of sorts, although whether it is sexual tension, or merely tension, is open for debate. None the less, something definitely began to heat up behind the well-starched exteriors of the duelling psychiatrists, and one of television's strangest romances soon developed. True, Lilith was briefly inclined to lust for Sam Malone, but Frasier is now her one true love: they moved in together, got married, and finally had a baby, becoming somewhat trendily yuppified along the way. As for the trauma of childbirth: Frasier advised her to endure labor with "Gentle, loving thoughts." Lilith had other ideas:

"Novocaine! Codeine! Demerol! Whiskey! Rum! Knock me unconscious!" The actual delivery took place in a taxi, after Frasier and Sam abandoned her to tend to an unwed mother in the maternity ward.

In a memorable episode soon afterwards, Lilith became unhinged when her favorite laboratory rat dies. displacement? Postpartum anxiety? Leave it to the psychiatrists to decide; on *Cheers*, it was simply hilarious.

Beatrice "Bebe" Neuwirth is the daughter of an artist and a mathematician. Born and raised in Princeton, New Jersey, she started out as a dancer: "I went to New York to see 'Pippin,' and I thought, 'I can do that. I will dance like that on Broadway.' The only other thing I considered being besides dancing was being a veterinarian on the side." Her New York career started out in *A Chorus Line*, where she started in— of all places— the chorus, and went on to play several roles in succession in the popular musical. She won a Tony award for her part in *Sweet Charity* on Broadway. Married to director Paul Dorman, she believes that happiness lies in finding one's true calling:

"I think there are a lot of unhappy people in this country because they're not doing what they want to do. It starts out with yourself, and if you're not true to your own love, then everything you do is altered by that.'

She is, however, aware of her own personal limitations, however slight: "I think too much. . . my mouth doesn't move. My mind goes so fast, and I have so many things jumbled, and I can't get anything to come out. . .

"On the one hand I think, '[People] can think whatever the hell they want [about me]. On the other hand, I think, 'Gee, I don't want them to think *this*,' or 'It would be nice if they thought *that*.' I don't try to lead my life for other people, and I don't think anyone should."

To facilitate working on *Cheers*, Bebe Neuwirth has taken up lodgings in Los Angeles. "I live in an apartment that is really nice, very light, and it's got windows on all sides. In New York, I have two windows on an air shaft. This place is like a treehouse."

On her own work, she observes, "I'd just like to do good work with good people, and if that happens in a theater on Broadway or if that happens in a small theater somewhere, that's fine, wherever."

So far, Bebe Neuwirth *has* done good work with good people, having been awarded an Emmy Award for Outstanding Supporting Actress in a Comedy Series this past year. She has also guest-starred on *Star Trek: The Next Generation* (as a sexually inquisitive alien who pursues Commander Riker), and recently appeared as Lilith Sternin-Crane (along with Kelsey Grammer as Frasier) on an episode of *Wings*. She most recently had a small role in the movie *Bugsy* as an Italian countess who has an affair with Bugsy Siegel.

THE STORIES

The ensemble cast of CHEERS interact in varied and complex ways with some action beginning in one episode only to be pursued in a later one. The events of one storyline often effect those of another. Forewith is a complex guide through the lives of the characters that populate a bar called Cheers.

Top, left to right: Rhea Perlman, Woody Harrelson, John Ratzenberger, Kirstie Alley and George Wendt.

Bottom: Ted Danson and Kelsey Grammer

SEASON ONE

(1982-1983)

NOTE: Episodes are listed alphabetically for each season in their original network broadcast order. Episode numbers indicate the order in which the episodes were filmed.

Ted Danson, Kelsey Grammer, John Ratzenberger and George Wendt

A. Episode One

Give Me a Ring Sometime

Written by Les and Glen Charles; Directed by Jim Burrows

Guest Starring: Michael McGuire (Sumner Sloan), Ron Frazier (Ron), John P. Navin (Boy)

The one that started it all. Diane Chambers arrives at Cheers with her fiance, Sumner Sloan. Diane was his teacher assistant before the two of them fell in love and is anticipating a trip to the Caribbean where she and Sumner will be married. Sumner leaves her at the bar so that he can go to his ex-wife's house to retrieve a very special wedding ring. Time passes, the minutes turning into hours, and Diane eventually realizes that Sumner has gotten back together with the former Mrs. Sloan. Now is a turning point in her life, and Diane must assess where she is going as a human being. Getting a job at Cheers may be the ticket to self-awareness, so she accepts Sam's offer to make her a waitress. This despite the fact that Sam only made the offer out of pity. Needless the say, the sparks immediately begin to fly.

B. Episode Two

Sam's Women

Written by Earl Pomerantz; Directed by James Burrows

Guest Starring: Donna McKechnie (Debra), Donnelly Rhodes (Leo Metz), Angela Aames (Brandee)

As Diane slips into the routine of Cheers, she quickly finds herself repulsed at the type of women that Sam has one-night-stands with. These women are beautiful, to be sure, but, in Diane's estimation, are empty-headed. Sam chooses to ignore her until a beautiful, well-endowed blonde named Brandee arrives. He starts to make his move on her, but is stopped by memories of Diane's previous comments. He debates whether or not the women he pursues are shallow, and concludes that he doesn't care! Ultimately he decides that what Diane thinks doesn't matter and makes his move. Unfortunately, Brandee has already met someone else. In a last ditch effort to impress Diane, Sam brings his ex-wife, Debra, into the bar. Intellectually, Diane blows her away, driving home her opinion of Sam's women.

NOTE: This episode was the first and last that made reference to Sam's ex-wife. Incidentally, Debra was portrayed by Donna McKechnie, who got her big break as Roxanne Drew on the ABC soap opera *Dark Shadows* and starred on Broadway in Bob Fosse's *A Chorus Line*.

C. Episode Four

The Tortelli Tort

Written by Tom Reeder; Directed by James Burrows

Guest Starring: John Fiedler (Fred), Ron Karobatsos (Ed Kellner), Stephen Keep (Dr. Gordon)

Upon arriving at Cheers, Ed Kellner shoots his mouth off with anti-Red Sox slurs. This infuriates everyone with the exception of Sam. Kellner then makes cracks about Sam's bouts with the bottle. Carla snaps and lets loose with her own verbal assault, which upsets Sam even more than the things that Kellner said. It's his feeling that Carla needs to see a psychiatrist to learn to control her temper. To this end, he brings one to the bar, and it's hysterical to watch Carla behave like the sweetest little waitress you'd want to tip.

D. Episode Five

Sam at Eleven

Written by Les and Glen Charles; Directed by James Burrows

Guest Starring: Fred Dryer (Dave Richards), Harry Anderson (Harry Gillies), Rick Dees (Young Guy), Julie Brown (Cathy)

Sam, who has no problem in the ego department, is delighted when former team-mate Dave Richards, who has recently become a TV sportscaster, decides to come to cheers and interview Sam for his Whatever Happened To.... series. To all the regulars this seems like a great opportunity to get Sam and Cheers some exposure, but Diane isn't so convinced. It's her feeling that any sports figure who sits around talking about his former glory days is a device that will not inspire awe from the audience, but, rather, sympathy. Sam, naturally, doesn't agree with this and is more than happy to do the interview. Unfortunately (and not for the last time), Diane proves to be correct. In the middle of the interview, Dave is told that he has a shot at getting a one-on-one with tennis star John McEnroe. Now *this* is news, and all the incentive he needs to leave. Sam is crushed and Diane tries to massage his ego.

NOTE: This is the first time we get the feeling that something could happen between Sam and Diane. Also, Fred Dryer, who portrayed Dave Richards, would go on two seasons later to star in *Hunter.* In addition, Harry Anderson, who has a small part as conman Harry Gillies, moved on to the ensemble comedy, *Night Court.*

E. Episode Seven

The Coach's Daughter

Written by Ken Estin; Directed by James Burrows

Guest Starring: Allyce Beasley (Lisa Pantusso), Philip Charles MacKenzie (Roy), Tim Cunningham (Chuck)

The arrival of Lisa Pantusso is nothing but joy for Coach. He hasn't seen his daughter in some time. Unfortunately, his joy turns to sorrow once he meets Roy, her fiance, and a real low-life who treats her like dirt. To make matters worse, he is using her to improve his own career, and readily admits this. Coach is at a loss. Why would this woman accept someone so obviously wrong for her? Finally, he sits down with Lisa and they have a heart-to-heart talk. Lisa admits that she's with Roy because she's not getting any younger and that she hasn't had much luck with men. Here, at least, is someone willing to be with her. It's a truly touching scene, but Coach, with Sam's help, manages to help Lisa see the fact that marrying Roy is not such a hot idea.

NOTE: Lisa Pantusso was portrayed by Allyce Beasley, who went on to play secretary Agnes DiPesto in the Bruce Willis/Cybill Shepard-starrer, *Moonlighting.*

F. Episode Eight

Any Friend of Diane's

Written by David Isaacs and Ken Levine; Directed by James Burrows

Guest Starring: Julia Duffy (Rebecca Prout), Macon McCalman (Darrell Stabell)

Rebecca Prout is just coming off of a failed relationship with an intellectual. When she arrives at Cheers, she confides to Diane that she's looking for someone with little or no brain power to be with; someone earthy. Eventually her line of vision locks on Sam, and she's convinced that he's the kind of guy she's looking for. This obviously affects Diane, who has developed some sort of feeling for Sam but refuses to admit it, and she does everything she can to prevent a date from being made. Despite her best attempts, the two do go out, but it turns out that Diane has nothing to worry about.

NOTE: Julia Duffy who guest starred as Rebecca Prout, went on to star in the CBS sitcom, *Newhart*.

G. Episode Thirteen

Friends, Romans and Accountants

Written by Ken Levine and David Isaacs; Directed by James Burrows

Guest Starring: James Read (H.W. Sawyer)

Norm has been made the chairman of his company's annual party, and as such decides he has to impress his boss, H.W. Sawyer. To this end, he plans a toga party, thinking that it will result in a party that no one will forget. In a certain sense he's right. He is the only one who shows up wearing a toga. Things get worse when Sawyer's date cancels out and, hoping to avoid a total disaster, Norm goes to Diane and begs that she serve as a stand in. Diane has no intention of doing so, until she sees the suave and great looking Sawyer, and is completely swept up by him. Sam is filled with jealousy, but feels that it wouldn't be macho to step up and do anything about his feelings. Then Sawyer tries to get his way with Diane and it's Norm who steps forward to tell his boss off. Putting it mildly, the night is *not* a wild success.

H. Episode Six

Truth or Consequences

Written by Ken Levine and David Isaacs; Directed by James Burrows

Guest Starring: Jack Knight (Jack)

Through the first six episodes, audiences have witnessed the fact that Carla and Diane have had nothing kind to say to each other. In Truth or Consequences, they call a truce from the verbal jabs. In a sense, this is a relief to Diane who is desperate for a friend and confidante. Carla, seeming to open up to her for the first time, confesses a story about one of her many pregnancies, but swears Diane to secrecy. So terrible is this burden, that Diane eventually feels as though she must discuss it with someone. Once this happens, Carla finds out and then lets her in on the fact that the story was just that: a story. She knew that Diane couldn't keep it to herself. Feeling used and manipulated, Diane verbally fights back and soon things are right back to where they originally were!

I. Episode Ten

Coach Returns to Action

Written by Earl Pomerantz; Directed by James Burrows

Guest Starring: Murphy Cross (Nina Bradshaw)

Despite the fact that it's been a while since Coach has been out on a date, he finds himself attracted to his neighbor, Ninda Bradshaw. This beautiful woman visits Cheers often, and is often pursued by Sam but without success. Coach would love to ask her out on a date, but he feels totally inhibited. Diane tries to convince him that all he has to do is ask her for a date and that she'll probably say yes, but Coach is still hesitant. Next, Diane goes to Sam and asks that he not pursue Nina, but she refuses to tell him why as it would betray Coach's secret feelings. Not understanding why she's making this request, Sam proceeds as usual. Surprisingly, Nina expresses her disinterest in Sam and, instead, lets Coach know that she cares about him. Sam is stunned.

J. Episode Nine

Endless Slumber

Written by Sam Simon; Directed by James Burrows

Guest Starring: Christopher McDonald (Rick Walker), Anne Haney (Miss Gilder)

Rick Walker, a pitcher for the Red Sox, comes to Cheers totally dejected. He has fallen into a slump as of late, and the fans have truly turned against him (as is the wont of fans). He begs Sam to loan him his lucky bottlecap. Although reluctant to do so, Sam agrees. This seems to have the desired effect, as Rick's luck made a sudden swing in a positive direction. Unfortunately, Sam's goes instantly bad. Diane comes to him and tries to make him realize that a little bottlecap could have nothing whatsoever to do with the up or down side of a person's life. Sam opens up to her, explaining why it's so significant to him and how, for whatever reasons, it played a role in getting him away from his alcoholic state of mind.

K. Episode Three

One For the Book

Written by Katherine Green; Directed by James Burrows

Guest Starring: Ian Wolfe (Buzz Crowder), Boyd Godwell (Kevin)

Kevin is a young man about to enter the monastery, who comes to Cheers to enjoy his first and last fling with a bottle. What he never expects is that the alcohol unlocks his inhibitions and hormones, resulting in his coming on like some kind of Casanova. His first target is Diane, and when he realizes what he tried to do, he comes to the conclusion that he is not ready to become a monk. Diane becomes very full of herself while at the same time inflicting a self-imposed head trip over being the one

who has taken this man from God. Occuring simultaneously is the arrival of a World War I pilot named Buzz Crawder, who is there for the six decade reunion of the 22nd Brigade's victory. Unfortunately, it seems that he is the only member still alive.

L. Episode Twelve

The Spy Who Came in For a Cold One

Written by David Lloyd; Directed by James Burrows

Guest Starring: Ellis Rabb (Eric Finch)

Eric Finch, a sophisticated and debonair Englishman, has been coming in to Cheers for quite some time. He tells exciting stories about his adventures as a secret agent during World War II. He manages to capture the imagination of everyone in the bar with the exception of—naturally—Diane, who feels compelled to point out where his version of history has obvious holes in it that differ from the way things really happened. Dejected and embarrassed, the man leaves the bar. Sam is furious that Diane felt she had to burst Finch's bubble and feelings of self worth. Consumed with guilt, Diane goes after him and brings him back, hoping to prove that he doesn't have to resort to fantasy to create an interesting life for himself.

NOTE: With Diane's whole general attitude, has anyone considered that her personality would be perfect for *The Odd Couple's* Felix Unger? For that matter, Sam would probably get along great with Oscar Madison. Anyway, just a thought....

M. Episode Sixteen

Now Pitching, Sam Malone

Written by Ken Levine and David Isaacs; Directed by James Burrows

Guest Starring: Barbara Babcock

(Lana Marshall), Rick Hill (Tibor Svet-kovic), Paul Vaughn (Paul)

When the beautiful and sexy Lana Marshall, a TV commercial agent, arrives at Cheers, she immediately locks her sights on Sam. It's her belief that he can be a big star in the world of commercial spokesmen. This thrills Sam, who is secretly desperate to be in the spotlight again after several years of retirement from the Red Sox. We eventually learn that Lana has a history of relationships with young athletes and she wants Sam to be her next conquest. Their relationship moves to the sexual and Diane tries to make him realize that he's being used as a sex object. At first Sam doesn't mind, but he eventually realizes that he doesn't like to be used sexually. It is obvious that Sam has double standards.

N. Episode Eleven

Let Me Count the Ways

Written by Heide Perlman; Directed by James Burrows

Guest Starring: Mark King (Marshall Lipton), Jack Knight (Jack)

Diane is devastated. Her cat, Elizabeth Barrett Browning (who else would give a cat that name?), has died and she is having a difficult time dealing with it. Going to work, she tries to get sympathy from her friends, but it seems that no one gives a damn. They are all more concerned with the game being played on television than with her feelings. Amazed, Diane starts to wonder if these people who she thought were her friends are actually anything more than just co-workers. Later, she and Sam have a moment alone, where she cries out that she was a lonely child that was always picked on. *That's* the reason she grew so attached to the animal, and why it hurts so badly now that it's gone. Sam tells a story about his own past, and somehow it makes her feel better.

O. Episode Fourteen

Father Knows Last

Written by Heide Perlman; Directed by James Burrows

Guest Starring: Mark King (Marshall Lipton)

Carla, who plainly admits that she has no problem conceiving children, finds herself pregnant again, this time with child number four. Being a divorced mother, she feels that she can't raise all these children by herself and so decides that she's going to get a responsible man to play father. She turns to a man named Marshall Lipton, who she did have relations with, and tells him that he's the father. He is delighted and will do the right thing. Once he excitedly leaves Cheers, Carla gloats to anyone who will listen that she tricked the man. Diane is aghast. How can she do such a thing to a man who would be so willing to face up to his responsibilities? Eventually this gets through to Carla who has a change of heart and tells Marshall the truth. There is no marriage.

P. Episode Fifteen

The Boys in the Bar

Written by Ken Levine and David Isaacs; Directed by James Burrows

Guest Starring: Alan Autry (Tom Jackson), Rick Dees (Rick), Julie Brown (Cathy), Jack Knight (Jack), Paul Vaughn (Paul)

Sam, who revels in his sports past, is delighted when he's asked by former roommate and teammate Tom Jackson to host a party at Cheers in honor of the man's newly published autobiography. Naturally he says yes, and starts making all of the preparations. *Then* he learns that Jackson, with whom Sam had spent years chasing women, is coming out of the closet, announcing to the world that he is really a homo-sexual. Just as one would assume, Sam has a difficult time dealing with this revelation, particularly when several reporters, who know that the party for the book is being held at Cheers, start implying that Sam and Tom might be more than just friends. Diane believes that Sam should stand by his friend, while Norm, Cliff and the rest of the Cheers regulars aren't so sure if they like the idea of this new clientele of customer.

NOTE: The episode title is a parody of *The Boys in the Band,* a play and film dealing openly with homosexuality.

Q. Episode Seventeen

Diane's Perfect Date

Written by David Lloyd; Directed by James Burrows

Guest Starring: Gretchen Corbett, Derek McGrath (Andy), Doug Sheehan (Walter)

Sam and Diane get into one of their typical superiority spats, with each other criticizing the others' choice in dating material. They agree to find each other the perfect date. Feeling that he and Diane would be perfect for each other, he assumes that Diane won't be able to come up with anyone. Sam doesn't take this little wager seriously, but then Diane introduces him to her beautiful friend Gretchen, who has an intense love for sports. Realizing he's in big trouble, Sam desperately tries to find the perfect date for Diane, and pays Andy, who's hanging out in Cheers' poolroom, to play date. Sam thinks that solves everything, until everyone learns that Andy is actually a paroled murderer. One can assume that this doesn't exactly light Diane's romantic fires.

R. Episode Nineteen

No Contest

Written by Heide Perlman; Directed by James Burrows

Guest Starring: Tim O'Neill (Himself), Charlie Stavola (Emcee), Renee Gentry (Yvonne), Tessa Richarde (Bonnie), Sharon Peters (Jocelyn), Paul Vaughn (Paul), Daryl Roach (Judge #1), Bob Ari (Judge #2), James Sherwood (Judge #3)

Believing he's doing the right thing, Sam enters a photo of Diane into the Miss Boston Barmaid contest, which will be held at Cheers. At first put off by the very notion of such exploitation, Diane eventually has a change of hearts and agrees to be a part of the contest, which is thrilling to Sam. Thrilling until he finds a portion of her planned speech, from which he learns that Diane is planning on denouncing the whole idea of beauty contests to the Boston media. This was *not* the kind of publicity that Sam had originally hoped for. Diane is intent on sticking to her guns until she wins the contest and learns what the grand prize is. Suddenly the situation isn't so bad after all.

S. Episode Eighteen

Pick a Con....Any Con

Written by David Angel; Directed by James Burrows

Guest Starring: Harry Anderson (Harry), Reid Shelton (George)

Everyone at Cheers is shocked to learn that Coach is $8,000 in debt from playing gin with his friend George Wheeler, whose crookedness is obvious to all but Coach. Believing his friend is being conned, Sam bails Harry, his own personal favorite conman, out of jail and puts a personal con into effect. It seems like a great idea, until Harry starts losing and then the fear mounts that the two conmen are working together. Thankfully, Harry proves virtuous, and beats Wheeler.

T. Episode Twenty

Someone Single, Someone Blue

Written by David Angel; Directed by James Burrows

Guest Starring: Glynis Johns (Helen Chambers), Duncan Ross (Boggs), Dean Dittman (Harrison Fiedler)

Diane's mother, Helen, comes to Cheers to drop the bombshell: if Diane doesn't get married within 24 hours, Helen will lose the inheritance left to her by Diane's late father. We learn that a very specific clause in his will decreed that Diane must be married by the 10th anniversary of the man's death, or the estate will cut off Helen. Diane is appalled by such barbaric ideas, but then learns that her mother is taking the whole thing very seriously. Out of desperation and love for her mother, Diane comes up with a business proposition by which she would marry Sam. A loophole in the will is enough to stop the marriage from going through.

U. Episode Twenty One

Show Down—Part I

Written by Glen and Les Charles; Directed by James Burrows

Guest Starring: George Ball (Derek), Alan Koss (Alan), Paul Vaughn (Paul), Deborah Shelton (Debbie)

Sam's brother Derek shows up, and immediately charms everyone at the bar, particularly Diane. At the same time, all of Sam's insecurities rise to the surface as he has spent most of his life feeling inferior to his brother, who is known around the globe as a trend-setting international lawyer. Diane is attracted to Derek, but has feelings of her own for Sam. She hopes that he will be moved to jealousy by the attention that Derek is playing to her. Unfortunately Sam decides to keep his feelings bottled up, and the episode ends with Derek asking Diane to fly away with him for the weekend.

NOTE: Deborah Shelton who has a small role in the episode, is perhaps best known for her role in Brian Depalma's *Body Double* and as a recurring character on the CBS prime time soap, *Dallas*.

V. Episode Twenty Two

Show Down—Part II

Written by Glen and Les Charles; Directed by James Burrows

Guest Starring: George Ball (Derek), Tim Cunningham (Chuck), Alan Koss (Alan), Paul Vaughn (Paul), Lois De Banzie (Lois), Helen Page Camp (Helen), Peggy Kubena (Cindy)

While Diane continues to date Derek, Sam immerses himself in a very active social life, doing his best to take his mind off of her. Things culminate when Derek asks her to leave this life and come to him in Europe. Diane gives this serious consideration, but realizes that her feelings for Sam are too strong. She can't go with him.

SEASON TWO

(1983-84)

Ted Danson and Rhea Perlman

A. Episode Twenty Three

Power Play

Written by Glen and Les Charles; Directed by James Burrows

Following the events of Show Down, Sam and Diane decide to investigate their strong feelings for each other. All the other series regulars think that this is a ridiculous, and in Carla's mind, repulsive idea. One night, Diane invites Sam to her apartment but instead of making love, they make war because of Sam's generally sarcastic attitude. Dejected and angry with himself, Sam goes back to Cheers where everyone blames themselves for what happened. They feel that their barbed comments played a role in the bad turn of events. Surprisingly it's Carla who offers Sam some advice on how to rectify the situation.

B. Episode Twenty Five

Little Sister Don't Cha

Written by Heide Perlman; Directed by James Burrows

Guest Starring: Paul Vaughn (Paul)

Before going into the hospital to give birth, Carla gets her sister Annette to fill in for her at Cheers. At first, Annette seems to be the exact opposite of Carla, quiet, sweet and very shy. But then, suddenly, she starts flirting with all the men and comes on to absolutely everyone. It gets so bad that Cliff thinks he's falling in love with her and wants to ask Annette to marry him. Norm takes it upon himself to set things straight, and everyone patiently awaits Carla's return to the bar.

NOTE: Rhea Perlman, who is married to actor-director Danny DeVito, played the dual role of Carla and Annette in this episode.

C. Episode Twenty Seven

Personal Business

Written by Tom Reederd; Directed by James Burrows

While Norm is seeking another woman to fill in for Vera, from whom he has separated (Hey, Norm, how'ya gonna meet someone sitting on that bar stool?), Carla starts complaining that Sam is playing favorites with Diane because she's his girlfriend. To combat this, Diane gets a dream job in an art gallery, feeling that this is her true call in life. Things go down hill, however, when her new employer calls Sam for a personal reference and reveals that he would love to sleep with Diane. It's only a short matter of time before Diane comes back to Cheers.

D. Episode Twenty Four

Homicidal Ham

Written by David Lloyd; Directed by James Burrows

Guest Starring: Derek McGrath (Andy), Paul Vaughn (Paul), Alan Koss (Alan), Drew Snyder (Phil), Severn Darden (Professor Dewitt)

Andy, the poor slob from episode number seventeen, Diane's Perfect Date, returns to the lives of the Cheers crowd. Having a difficult time adapting to the world outside of prison, Andy starts committing petty crimes in the hopes that he will be arrested again. Taking pity on him, Diane tries to convince him that life on the outside can be good, and she encourages him to pursue his dream of acting. Sam is against the whole idea, but Diane won't listen to him. Instead, she serves as Andy's drama coach and then convinces Sam to allow the two of them to perform a scene from *Othello* at Cheers. Sam, finally convinced that Diane has done the right thing, gives his blessing to the whole idea and things seem to be going great. But *then*....Andy, who has developed a crush on Diane, sees her kissing Sam and his mind snaps. During the strangulation scene they're acting, he actually starts choking the life out of Diane until Sam pulls him off. Andy gets his wish and goes back to jail.

NOTE: Derek McGrath, who portrayed Andy, is a series regular on the syndicated action/adventure series, *My Secret Identity*. Science fiction fans will recognize Severn Darden, who portrays acting instructor Professor Dewitt, as Chief Kolp in the films *Conquest of the Planet of the Apes* and *Battle for the Planet of the Apes*.

E. Episode Twenty Eight

Sumner's Return

Written by Michael J. Weithorn; Directed by James Burrows

Guest Starring: Michael McGuire (Sumner Sloan)

Having been plagued with guilt since he first left Diane at Cheers about a year earlier, Sumner Sloan shows up at the tavern, claiming to be devastated over the idea that Diane, someone he had cared for so much, would hate him. To rectify this situation, he suggests that Diane and Sam go out with he and his wife to patch things up. Despite how bizarre this idea might be, Diane decides to go through with it in order to show Sumner that she bounced back from being dropped by him. Sam, meanwhile, has to cope with the idea of spending an evening with three intellectuals, and to this end he follows Cliff's advice and starts reading *War and Peace*.

F. Episode Twenty Nine

Affairs of the Heart

Written by Heide Perlman; Directed by James Burrows

Guest Starring: Don Amendolia (Hank Sweeney)

Carla is immediately suspicious when Hank Sweeney, seemingly a perfectly normal, nice guy, shows an attraction for her. So fearful is she of being rejected, that she decides to test Hank every chance that she gets. Sam tries to get her to loosen up and not be so negative all the time. His words finally get through to her, and Carla decides that this could indeed be Mr. Right. After being begged, Diane agrees to let her and Hank use her apartment so that they can consummate their relationship. No sooner have the couple departed Cheers, than Coach makes mention of the fact that Hank has a heart condition. Excitement of the carnal kind could kill him.

G. Episode Thirty Two

Old Flames

Written by David Angell; Directed by James Burrows

Guest Starring: Fred Dryer (Dave Richards), Elizabeth McIvor (Didi)

Dave Richards, who first appeared in episode five, Sam at Eleven, has recently gotten divorced and decides to hang out with his old buddy Sam Malone and pick up women. Sam points out that he and Diane are now a couple. Dave responds that he can break them up within 24 hours. Diane is convinced that this isn't possible, but Sam is concerned. Dave is not the kind of guy to make false statements. As one would expect, the harder they attempt to get along, the more they fight. Things really reach a head when Diane asks Sam to throw away his little black book. If he loves her as much as he claims to, then there's no reason for him to keep it. Just when it seems that things couldn't get any worse, Dave shows up with two beautiful women and asks Sam to take one of them home. He reluctantly agrees, and then she starts coming on to him. Sam avoids temptation and he and Diane remain together.....for the moment.

H. Episode Twenty Six

Manager Coach

Written by Earl Pomerantz; Directed by James Burrows

Guest Starring: Herb Mitchell (Mort Sherwin), Elliot Scott (Pee Wee)

When Coach is made the manager of a little-league team, everyone thinks that it's the best thing that could have happened to him. But then something strange happens. The usually quiet, befuddled and lovable coach is replaced with a madman who wants his team to win no matter what the cost. He gets so carried away that you would think this was a professional ball team. The kids can only take his strictness and attitude so much, and decide that they're going to fire him. Sam has a heart to heart with Coach, who finally sees the error of his ways and lightens up on the children.

I. Episode Thirty One

They Called Me Mayday

Written by David Angell; Directed by James Burrows

Guest Starring: Dick Cavett (Himself), Walter Olkewicz (Wally Bodell)

When Dick Cavett comes into Cheers for a drink, he's surprised to discover that Sam Malone is the owner. Being a tremendous Red Sox fan, he's extremely impressed and thinks that Sam should write his memoirs, which Ca-

vett will then submit to his publisher. Diane, who considers herself the intellectual of the group, is extremely jealous over the idea that Sam, someone who is monosyllabic, should get this opportunity when she hasn't. Believing that Sam needs all the help that he can get, Diane agrees to help him and, together, they write the first 50 pages, designing it in such a way that it will appeal to the intellectual Cavett. Unfortunately it is so stuffy and thick with prose, that neither Cavett nor his publisher think that there's a market for it. A concurrent plot is Norm running into Wally Bodell, who had pursued his wife, Vera, while they were all still in high school. Learning that Norm and Vera are separated, Wally decides that this will be a great opportunity make up for the past and he sets about pursuing her again. This makes Norm realize how much he really cares about her.

J. Episode Thirty Three

How Do I Love Thee.....Let Me Call You Back

Written by Earl Pomerantz; Directed by James Burrows

In an effort to surprise Sam, Diane comes into Cheers with some tickets for a sold out boxing match. Filled with excitement he says, Oh, Diane, I love you. This is a stunning moment for Diane, who takes his statement on face value and is completely moved. Sam, nervous at the inherent commitment, tries backing away from it, noting that what he said wasn't something she should take quite so seriously. Now upset, Diane thinks that it would be best that they not see each other for about a week so that they can evaluate the feelings they have for each other and the direction they think their relationship should go. In seven days they will get together and share the notes they've made for each other which are supposed to express their deepest feelings. Diane comes back with a ream of paper while Sam hasn't bothered to write anything down, thinking they would just talk about their relationship.

K. Episode Thirty Seven

Just Three Friends

Written by David Lloyd; Directed by James Burrows

Guest Starring: Markie Post (Heather Landon)

Heather Landon, Diane's best friend since childhood, decides that she's going to move to Boston. Wanting to make Heather feel at home, Diane desires that she, Heather and Sam all be good friends. When Diane's not around, Heather begins flirting with Sam and when he tells Diane about this, she brushes it off as Sam's ego being in overdrive. Heather excuses her flirting as being nothing more than a tease, but the reality becomes apparent when the trio get together for dinner at Diane's apartment. Heather practically leaps across the table to attack Sam.

NOTE: Heather Landon is portrayed by Markie Post, best known for her role as Christine Sullivan in *Night Court*.

L. Episode Thirty

Where There's a Will....

Written by Nick Arnold; Directed by James Burrows

Guest Starring: George Gaynes (Malcolm Kramer), Alan Koss (Alan)

Told that he only has a short time to live, Cheers patron Malcolm Kramer comes to the bar hoping that the atmosphere will lift his spirits. It works and he's feeling much better. So grateful is he, that, as he leaves, he decides

that he's going to alter his will so that the Cheers regulars will receive $100,000 upon his death. The only drawback is that he doesn't specify how much will go to which particular person. This, of course, leads to a series of arguments over who should get the majority of the money, and in order to settle things, Coach is asked to bring Malcolm back to Cheers. Once he returns, Malcolm gives Sam all rights to the money so that he can distribute it in the manner he thinks most appropriate. Everyone goes crazy, trying to be Sam's best friend, and it's Diane's suggestion that Sam burn the will. As she sees it, it's the only way to make everyone normal again.

M. Episode Thirty Four

Battle of the Exes

Written by Ken Estin and Sam Simon; Directed by James Burrows

Guest Starring: Dan Hedaya (Nick Tortelli), Jean Kasem (Loretta)

Look up the word sleaze in the dictionary, and you'll find a photo of Nick Tortelli, Carla's ex-husband who, in Battle of the Exes, comes to Cheers with his soon-to-be bride, the airhead Loretta, to rub it in Carla's face that he's found a gorgeous new wife. Refusing to let him bother her, Carla decides to attend the wedding. She asks Sam to go along as her hunky date. Diane hates the idea, until she overhears Nick really putting Carla down. Following the wedding, Carla is depressed because Nick seems to have gotten his life back together, whereas she is still going nowhere. Sam provides the words that brighten her night.

NOTE: Dan Hedaya played another sleazy husband to perfection in the Coen Brothers film *Blood Simple*, and is currently appearing in *The Addams*

Family film as the Addams' sleazy, treacherous lawyer. Check out *Blood Simple*, however, for his greatest depths of sleaze. It's a classic, sadly underrated and overlooked.

N. Episode Thirty Six

No Help Wanted

Written by Max Tash; Directed by James Burrows

In desperate need of an accountant, Sam turns to the unemployed. Norm goes right to work and discovers that Sam is entitled to a $30,000 refund from the government. Believing that alcohol may have gone to Norm's head, Sam decides to have another accountant recheck the figures. Norm gets wind of this and is insulted, swearing to leave Cheers forever. Sam makes amends, despite the fact that there is no refund coming to him.

O. Episode Thirty Five

Coachie Makes Three

Written by Heide Perlman; Directed by James Burrows

Guest Starring: Eve Roberts (Katherine)

Coach is loved by everyone at Cheers, particularly Sam and Diane, but the old expression two is company, three's a crowd, bears its head in the relationship between the couple. As of late, Coach has been inviting himself over to Diane's apartment every night so that he can watch the late show with his two favorite people. Sam and Diane realize that the only way to get rid of Coach is to set him up with a woman of his own. That's exactly what they set out to do, with the usual *Cheers* results.

P. Episode Forty

Cliff's Rocky Romance

Written by David Lloyd; Directed by James Burrows

Guest Starring: Peter Iacangelo (Victor Shapone), Sam Scarber (Lewis)

A bully named Vic Shapone has grown tired of Cliff's constant droning about everything and nothing. The two get into one argument after another, culminating in Vic's challenging Cliff to a fight. Cliff declines, brushing the whole thing off as a joke, but Vic starts to humiliate him. For a while Cliff avoids Cheers, but finally decides to confront the situation, stating that the reason he didn't want to fight was because he's an expert in karate and was afraid he would cause some serious damage to the other man. Everyone at Cheers refuses to believe this, until Cliff provides an effective—though ultimately hysterical—demonstration.

Q. Episode Thirty Nine

Fortune and Men's Weights

Written by Heide Perlman; Directed by James Burrows

Having purchased an attractive antique weight/fortune teller machine, Coach brings it to Cheers as decoration. It's not long before everyone in the bar starts to believe that the device contains supernatural abilities. As proof, Norm asks for his fortune and is told in response, Your worst problem will be solved. Soon thereafter, he has a reconciliation with his wife, Vera. Diane scoffs the whole thing off as nothing more than a coincidence. To prove it, she uses the device herself and is told Deception in romance proves costly. Her mind moves to Sam, and she ponders the validity of the statement.

R. Episode Thirty Eight

Snow Job

Written by David Angell; Directed by James Burrows

As Washington's Birthday approaches, Carla takes great delight in informing Diane that this is the weekend that, traditionally, Sam and his buddies go skiing to pick up babes. Diane refuses to believe her, insisting that Sam will give up that yearly sojourn to spend time with his beloved. Sam dashes her confidence, however, when he comes up with an incredible lie to explain where he's going to be that weekend. Diane uses everything at her disposal to get Sam to admit the truth.

S. Episode Forty One

Coach Buries a Grudge

Written by David Lloyd; Directed by James Burrows

In what is actually a very touching episode of *Cheers,* Coach mourns the death of an old baseball buddy who recently died. He cherishes his memory of the man and is proud to have them for the rest of his life, until he learns that the deceased had tried to proposition Coach's wife decades earlier. Suddenly Coach is filled with venom, which is amplified when the rest of his old teammates arrive at the bar to toast his memory. Before Coach makes too big a scene, Diane, who was once a psychology major, tries to make him understand that he can't hold on to the hatred; that he should remember all of the good things. Coach at least had a wife, whereas this man died alone. Through role-playing, in which she plays his ex-wife and Sam plays the late friend, Coach sees the truth in her words.

T. Episode Forty Two

Norman's Conquest

Written by Lissa Levin; Directed by James Burrows

Guest Starring: Anne Schedeen (Emily Phillips)

Emily Phillips, a new client of Norm's, finds herself attracted to him. Norm starts to have palpitations over the idea. Everyone in the bar gives him pep talks to essentially go for it, but Diane insists that he think of Vera. The ribbing by the other Cheers patrons continues until Norm feels that he has no choice in the matter: he will sleep with Emily. He sets off for what's supposed to be a wild night of passion, and comes back to Cheers late in the evening, confessing to Sam that he couldn't go through with it. The thought of hurting Vera was just too much for him.

U. Episode Forty Three

I'll Be Seeing You—Part I

Written by Glen and Les Charles; Directed by James Burrows

Guest Starring: Christopher Lloyd (Phillip Semenko)

Sam innocently agrees to be interviewed as one of Boston's ten most eligible bachelors by a local magazine. The fact that Sam considers himself a bachelor is more than Diane can take, and she is absolutely furious with him. Not realizing that he had been insensitive to her feelings, Sam decides to make it up to her by having painter Phillip Semenko do a portrait of Diane. Eventually Semenko comes to Cheers dressed in a Arapaho ceremonial tunic, and it's obvious that he and Sam instantly dislike each other. Sam's feelings are accentuated when the painter tells Diane that he would like to capture her so-called tortured soul, which he blames on Sam. It is Semenko's hope that the portrait will be a catharsis that will separate her from Sam.

V. Episode Forty Four

I'll Be Seeing You—Part II

Written by Glen and Les Charles; Directed by James Burrows

Guest Starring: Christopher Lloyd (Phillip Semenko)

As Semenko paints Diane, he is unleashing a ceaseless attack on Sam, constantly reinforcing his belief that the couple are not fit for each other. These words seem to have the desired effect. By the time the portrait is done, Diane is actually concerned about the reality of her relationship with Sam. She rushes off to show it to Sam, and when he doesn't recognize the greatness in Semenko's work, Diane realizes that the two of them aren't right for each other and they break up.

SEASON THREE

(1984-1985)

John Ratzenberger, George Wendt and Woody Harrelson

A. Episode Forty Five

Rebound—Part I

Written by Glen and Les Charles; Directed by James Burrows

Guest Starring: Duncan Ross (Boggs)

A new season begins with the aftermath of the Sam and Diane breakup. Sam is drinking heavily again and is chasing women more than ever. Diane has just ended a self-imposed sentence at the Golden Brook Sanitarium, and has absolutely no intention of going back to Cheers. Then Coach shows up, describing how badly Sam has slipped. According to him, Diane *has* to come to Cheers to talk to him. Recognizing that Sam does indeed have a problem, she agrees to talk to him, but brings along her psychiatrist, Dr. Frasier Crane to help. What Sam doesn't know is that Diane and Frasier have become lovers.

NOTE: From this episode on, Kelsey Grammer would become a *Cheers* regular.

B. Episode Forty Six

Rebound—Part II

Written by Glen and Les Charles; Directed by James Burrows

Guest Starring: Kelsey Grammer (Dr. Frasier Crane)

Frasier Crane actually seems to be making some progress with Sam. Viewing this, Diane thinks that it's time Sam be told the truth about her and Frasier. Frasier is reluctant but tells Sam the news. It seems to have little effect on him. In fact, he seems to pity the psychiatrist. Later, a waitress quits Cheers and Coach sees this as a good opportunity to get Sam and Diane, who obviously still have feelings for each other, back together. He uses some psychology of his own (which is pretty amazing if you consider Coach's personality makeup) and convinces her that if she doesn't come back to work at the bar, Sam will turn back to the bottle. Frasier thinks her working there will be a wonderful mental reinforcement for her and her determination that she feels nothing for Sam. By episode's end, Diane is back in business at Cheers.

C. Episode Fifty One

I Call Your Name

Written by Peter Casey and David Lee; Directed by James Burrows

Guest Starring: Sam Scarber (Lewis)

A disgruntled Frasier shows up at Cheers, needing to talk to someone. In a sense, it's a mistake that he chooses Sam. It seems that Diane hasn't quite gotten over her feelings for Sam. When she's making love with Frasier, she calls out Sam's name. Just as one would assume, this does wonders for Sam's ego. Diane eventually finds out about the reason for his gloating and is furious. Then she meets with Sam in his office, admitting that there must still be something between them. The two of them lock in a passionate embrace and start kissing with all their heart. Then Diane smiles and moans, Oh, Frasier. Revenge is hers! Meanwhile, a subplot revolves around Cliff's turning in a thieving co-worker at the post office, and the man's attempt to get revenge.

D. Episode Fifty Six

Fairy Tales Can Come True

Written by Sam Simon; Directed by James Burrows

Guest Starring: Bernadette Birkett (Tinker Bell)

It looks like Cliff has finally gotten the opportunity for true love. At a Cheers

Halloween party, he's dressed as Ponce de Leon and meets a beautiful woman dressed as Tinkerbell. The two of them seem to be hitting it off great and make plans to go out on a date. However, insecurity starts to overwhelm Cliff when he starts wondering whether or not she'll like the real him Meanwhile, Frasier has to abruptly go out of town and asks Sam to escort Diane to a concert that the two of them were going to go to. Sam agrees, but it's only a short matter of time before both Frasier and Diane start to have second thoughts about the idea.

E. Episode Forty Eight

Sam Turns the Other Cheek

Written by David Lloyd; Directed by James Burrows

Guest Starring: Kim Lankford (Maxine), Carmen Argenziano (Marvin)

As much of a ladies man that people consider Sam to be, he operates under certain rules. One of them is to never date a married woman. Unfortunately, said rule is broken, albeit unknowingly, when he dates and sleeps with the lovely Maxine. Upon discovering the truth, he breaks off the relationship. Too late. . . Maxine's jealous husband, Marvin, shows up at Cheers, brandishing a gun. Sam talks the husband into giving him the gun and Sam puts it in his pocket. An instant later, the gun goes off, wounding Sam's behind. Embarrassed, he comes up with a wild story about armed robbers to tell the regular gang. Diane doesn't believe a word of it, and goes about uncovering the truth.

F. Episode Forty Nine

Coach in Love—Part I

Written by David Angell; Directed by James Burrows

Guest Starring: Betty Ford (Irene Blanchard), Ellen Regan (Sue Blanchard)

Sam is amazed that he can't get to first base with Sue Blanchard, while Coach seems to be doing great with her mother, Irene. In fact, it's easy to discern that the two of them are falling very deeply in love with each other and eventually they announce their plans to get married.

G. Episode Fifty

Coach in Love—Part II

Written by David Angell; Directed by James Burrows

Guest Starring: Betty Ford (Irene Blanchard)

Coach's wedding plans are going along smoothly, until the bride-to-be, Irene Blanchard, wins a two million dollar lottery. Suddenly she's no longer interested in Coach, but he simply doesn't grasp the subtle ways she tries to inform him. Blissful in his ignorance, Coach continues making the preparations. Sam and Diane try to make him understand the reality of the situation, but it's not an easy task to accomplish.

H. Episode Fifty Two

Diane Meets Mom

Written by David Lloyd; Directed by James Burrows

Guest Starring: Nancy Marchand (Hester Crane)

Frasier's mother, a well known psychologist in her own right, comes to town to meet the woman in her son's life. Everything seems to be going great as the trio come to Cheers for an after-dinner drink. Frasier excuses himself to the men's room and at that moment, Hester Crane leans over the table and states that Frasier has a brilliant future ahead of him that can be jeopardized by his relationship with Diane. In all seriousness, she warns Diane that if she continues to see Frasier, she'll kill her! Diane is stunned but can't react as Frasier approaches the table. Later, Diane tells Frasier what transpired, but he finds it difficult to believe. Laughing it off, he mentions it to his mother who is hurt by such an allegation. A moment or so later, however, she states to Diane that she owns a gun and will use it. It eventually comes down to Diane making Frasier choose between her and Hester, with Frasier ultimately siding with Diane. Hester is deeply hurt and admits that the only reason she's acting in such a way is that she's afraid of losing her son. A truce is worked out but we're still not convinced that Hester doesn't want to kill Diane.

I. Episode Forty Seven

An American Family

Written by Heide Perlman; Directed by James Burrows

Guest Starring: Dan Hedaya (Nick), Jean Kasem (Loretta)

The sleazy Nick Tortelli returns to Cheers, having just gotten married to Loretta, the woman we met in episode 34, Battle of the Exes. This time Nick has come to demand the custody of his and Carla's oldest son, Anthony. Everyone is stunned that Carla actually agrees to this without a fight. It's Diane who really tries to gain an understanding of why Carla is so willing to give in to Nick (she hates to admit it, but she finds him irresistible). Once this is done, everyone encourages Carla to find the strength to stand up to him and reclaim custody of their son.

NOTE: Some time after this episode aired, NBC offered viewers a spin-off series entitled *The Tortellis*. It died a quick death.

J. Episode Fifty Five

Diane's Allergy

Written by David Lloyd; Directed by James Burrows

In an effort to prove her love for Frasier, Diane agrees to move in to his apartment with him. Soon thereafter, she begins sneezing like crazy and develops a horrid allergy. Initially it's believed that she is allergic to his dog, Pavlov, and Sam agrees to take the dog in. It breaks Frasier's heart to give up his beloved pet, but his love for Diane outweighs all. Unfortunately, the allergy continues, with Diane's voice developing a squeaky twang to it. Diane and Frasier have no choice but to end the living arrangement. Frasier gets back his dog, Sam has a great time watching all of this, and the couple remain together. . . for now.

K. Episode Fifty Four

Peterson Crusoe

Written by David Angell; Directed by James Burrows

Norm's world is suddenly thrown upside down when a chest x-ray uncovers a spot and he fears for his life. Re-evaluating his life, Norm realizes that there are still many things he wants to do before he dies. He starts giving away many of his possessions and eventually bids farewell to the Cheers gang as he announces that he's going to sail to Bora Bora, something he's wanted to do all of his life. Weeks pass and Cheers receives periodic post cards from Norm. He claims to be living out the adventures he's always dreamed of. The truth is that he's actually living in the Cheers store room, too embarrassed to show his face for fear he'll be made fun of for not going through with his proclamation. Incidentally, the spot on Norm's x-ray turns out to be nothing.

L. Episode Fifty Three

A Ditch in Time

Written by Ken Estin; Directed by James Burrows

Guest Starring: Carol Kane (Amanda)

When an attractive woman named Amanda comes into Cheers, Sam immediately starts to hit on her and she returns the flirtation. Diane is horrified because this woman is a member of her therapy group and has been in one bad compulsive relationship after another.and tends to get suicidal. Sam refuses to believe that Diane's warnings are serious, feeling that she's actually jealous but won't admit it. Soon he discovers the truth when Amanda invites her mother to Boston to meet the man she's going to marry.

NOTE: Guest star Carol Kane, besides her extensive feature film roles, was a semi-regular on the TV series *Taxi,* cast as Latka's girlfriend, Simka, and most has most recently been a part of the *American Dreamer* cast.

M. Episode Fifty Seven

Whodunit?

Written by Tom Reeder; Directed by James Burrows

Guest Starring: James Karen (Dr. Ludlow)

One of the men responsible for Frasier's career, Dr. Ludlow, pays a visit to Cheers and (amazingly) is smitten by Carla, immediately asking her out for a date. She accepts the invitation and the two engage in an incredible romance. Not to do anything too unexpected, Carla announces that she is pregnant with child number six. Ludlow proposes to her in order to do the right thing, but she turns him down.

NOTE: Character actor James Karen (Dr. Ludlow) is undoubtedly best known to television viewers as The Pathmark Man. He has also been in *F.I.S.T., Poltergeist, Return of the Living Dead* and *Wall Street.*

N. Episode Fifty Eight

The Heart is a Lonely Snipehunter

Written by Heide Perlman; Directed by James Burrows

Both Diane and Frasier are constantly bemoaning the fact that he is treated like an outsider at Cheers; that the regulars virtually ignore him and sling insults all the time. Perhaps out of guilt, Sam and the others invite Frasier on a fishing trip with them. This is a thrilling prospect for Frasier, who finally feels as though he belongs somewhere. So happy is he, that he is oblivious to the trick being pulled on him when the guys ask him to go out on a snipe hunt. As soon as he does this, they abandon him and head back to Cheers. There, a furious Diane gives them a piece of her considerable mind and the usual comedy of errors ensues.

O. Episode Sixty One

King of the Hill

Written by Elliot Shoeman; Directed by James Burrows

Guest Starring: Playboy Playmates (Themselves)

When Sam left the Red Soxs, he swore that he would never partake in one of those infamous old-timers games in which the once mighty gather together again to show that they've still got it. He has second thoughts, however, when he learns that the opposing team in this game for charity will be the Playboy Playmates. How could he be expected to resist such a temptation? Unfortunately he infuriates everyone when instinct takes over and he plays to win, thus preventing the Playmates from running around the bases.

P. Episode Sixty-Two

Teacher's Pet

Written by Tom Reeder; Directed by James Burrows

Although he tries to keep it a secret from the others at Cheers, Sam has been secretly attending night school with Coach in an effort to earn his high school diploma. Eventually the news does slip out and Diane thinks that it's absolutely wonderful, expressing her admiration for Sam's determination to better himself. Her mood brightens even more when she learns that both men are A students. This passes, however, when Coach makes a casual mentioning of the fact that he never sees Sam crack a book, while he himself has to study his brains out. Diane eventually learns that Sam is sleeping with his teacher and therefore is doing absolutely nothing to earn his grade. Diane appeals to him to be honest to himself above all others. What good is having a high school degree if it doesn't mean anything? Her words get through to him and Sam ends the affair with his teacher. He will have to pass the course on his own. Coach offers to help him study and he ends up with a D. There is some additional satisfaction in the fact that at episode's end he seems to know more state capitals than Diane does.

Q. Episode Sixty-Four

The Mail Goes to Jail

Written by David Lloyd; Directed by James Burrows

Cliff is feeling miserable and isn't so sure he'll be able to finish his route. Norm, out of friendship, offers to do it for him and Cliff hesitantly agrees. Shortly thereafter, Norm is arrested and charged with tampering with the mail. The arresting officer brings Norm to Cheers to get Cliff to tell the whole story, but, out of fear of losing his job, he denies any knowledge of what the man is talking about. Norm is taken to jail and Cliff is consumed with guilt. Deciding that his friendship with Norm is more important, he steps forward and tells the truth. Norm is freed and Cliff receives little more than a verbal warning from his superiors.

R. Episode Sixty-Six

Behind Every Great Man

Written by Ken Levine and David Isaacs; Directed by James Burrows

Guest Starring: Alison La Placa (Paula Nelson)

Reporter Paula Nelson is writing a story for *Boston Scene* magazine on the city's single scene, and is led to Cheers and Sam Malone. During the interview he comes across as his usual self-serving, I'm-the-answer-to-every-woman's-dreams attitude and she is immediately turned off by him and his shallowness. Determined to prove her wrong, Sam bones up on Impressionist art to prove he is an intellectual. He makes the mistake of asking Diane questions about the subject matter and revealing the knowledge he has thus far accumulated. Diane is convinced that Sam is trying to win her back. In an embarrassing conclusion in which she thinks he's taking her away for the weekend, she discovers the truth.

S. Episode Sixty-Five

If Ever I Would Leave You

Written by Ken Levine and David Isaacs; Directed by James Burrows

Guest Starring: Dan Hedaya (Nick Tortelli), Jean Kasem (Loretta Tortelli)

Nick Tortelli is thrown out of the house by Loretta, who claims that she wants a divorce. He shows up at Cheers and tries to convince Sam to give him a job and begs Carla to take him back. If she does, he'll be her slave forever. Carla is resistant to the idea, fearing that she'll be hurt again, but she is about to give in when Loretta arrives and tells Nick that she'll take him back.

T. Episode Sixty-Seven

The Executive's Executioner

Written by Heide Perlman; Directed by James Burrows

Guest Starring: Richard Roat (Mr. Heckt)

Norm's employer, Mr. Heckt, comes to Cheers and finds Norm goofing off, as has often been reported to him. He is about to fire him, when something about Norm comes across as very sympathetic and he comes up with an alternate idea. Norm can either be fired or accept a promotion to Executive Executioner. He will be the one who will fire executives. Needing the financial security, Norm comes up with a unique approach: those destined for the axe will come down to Cheers, Norm will cry for them and drop the bombshell. Things go well...in fact too well. The legend of Norm Peterson swiftly grows and all men sent to see him start to dread him as they would dread the Grim Reaper himself. Diane observes all of this and suggests that he quit, because his heart truly isn't into his job.

U. Episode Sixty-Three

Bar Bet

Written by Jim Parker; Directed by James Burrows

Guest Starring: Michael Richards (Eddie Gordon), Laurie Walters (Jacqueline Bisset)

The past finally catches up to Sam when old friend Eddie Gordon shows up. Eddie brings up a bet the two of them had made during Sam's days as an alcoholic. Sam agreed to be married to Jacqueline Bisset by midnight the following day or he will lose Cheers to Eddie. Feeling that honoring such a bet is the only thing he can do, Sam and the rest of the gang search high and low for a solution. Eventually they find a young woman named Jacqueline Bisset who finally agrees to marry Sam. Finally he decides that it isn't right and he backs out of the arrangement, deciding that if he has to lose the bar to Eddie it's something he'll have to learn how to live with. Eddie, recognizing the fact that Sam could have indeed fulfilled the bet (despite the fact that both of them knew they were talking about the actress), cancels out.

V. Episode Fifty-Nine

Cheerio Cheers

Written by Jim Parker; Directed by James Burrows

Is Diane leaving Cheers? That's the general feeling when Frasier is offered the opportunity to temporarily teach at the University of Bologna and he asks her to join him. Diane seriously considers this, although there is a part of her that wants Sam to step forward, declare his love for her, and insist that she stay in Boston with him. This little hope doesn't come true. Sam throws her a farewell party and doesn't seem to be bothered at all.

W. Episode Sixty Eight

The Bartender's Tale

Written by Sam Simon; Directed by James Burrows

Guest Starring: Lila Kaye (Lillian), Camilla More (Carolyn)

Needing to find a replacement for Diane, Sam starts interviewing potential waitresses, restricted by Carla's demands that it not be someone that Sam would be attracted to. She will *not* put up with another Diane type of relationship. Her prayers are apparently answered when Sam hires a proper English woman named Lillian. Unfortunately the woman's daughter, Carolyn, is quite beautiful but Sam is restricted from dating her by Carla's threat to quit. Things go typically insane when Lillian becomes convinced that Sam is lusting after her, while Carla gives Sam permission to pursue Carolyn, only to learn that the women abhors sex.

X. Episode Sixty-Nine

The Belles of St. Clete's

Written by Ken Estin; Directed by James Burrows

Guest Starring: Camilla Ashland (Drusilla DiMeglio)

While Diane and Frasier are getting on each other's nerves after so much close proximity, Carla is convinced that the teacher she always hated, Drusilla DiMeglio, has come to town and is frequenting Cheers. She plots revenge with her former schoolmates, but ends up liking the woman. Carla being the person she is, still extracts her vengeance without the woman even knowing it.

Y. Episode Sixty

Rescue Me

Written by Ken Estin; Directed by James Burrows

Guest Starring: Martin Ferrero (Walter)

While in Europe, Frasier proposes to Diane and he wants them to get married the following day. Rather than answer the question immediately, Diane excuses herself, goes to the telephone, and calls Sam. Once the connection is made, she tells him about what has transpired. Again—and this is obviously driving Diane crazy—he acts as though it doesn't mean anything to him. Instead of telling her that he loves her, Sam merely wishes her congratulations. Hurt, Diane goes to Frasier and tells him that she will marry him. Unbeknownst to her, Sam has boarded a plane to try and stop the wedding, but Diane has changed the ceremony's locale. This episode is the cliff-hanging third season finale.

SEASON FOUR

(1985-1986)

Ted Danson, Kelsey Grammer, John Ratzenberger and George Wendt

A. Episode Seventy

"Birth, Death, Love and Rice"

Written by Heide Perlman; Directed by James Burrows

Six months have passed since the conclusion of season three, when Sam flew to Italy in an effort to stop Diane from getting married. Unable to find her, he cames back to Cheers and immerses himself in life at the bar. In the meantime, we learn that Coach has passed away (due to the real-life death of actor Nicholas Colasanto). Shortly after this is discussed, farmboy Woody Boyd shows up at Cheers. He is a pen-pal of the Coach, who promised to show him the bar-tending ropes. Sam, feeling that this is at least an honest-to-God connection to Coach, hires Woody as his new bartender. Woody proves himself to be every bit as, shall we say, preoccupied as Coach in the brains department. Meanwhile, Frasier, on the verge of a nervous breakdown, shocks everyone by entering the bar, explaining that Diane left him at the alter and entered a convent to find inner peace. Sam goes to see Diane and convinces her that she would be better off back at Cheers. The two of them would just be friends. Diane agrees, though the two of them realize that their feelings for each other could bubble back to the surface.

B. Episode Seventy Two

"Woody Goes Belly Up"

Written by Heidi Perlman; Directed by James Burrows

Guest Starring: Amanda Wyss (Beth)

Depressed over his rejection from Diane, Frasier starts drinking too much and runs up a tremendous tab at Cheers. To work it off, he takes to sweeping up the bar. Meanwhile, Woody makes mention of the fact that he is homesick and everyone chips in to bring his girlfriend, Beth, to Boston. What we eventually learn is that the two of them have repressed their sexual appetite for each other by eating everything they can, and since being apart they've managed to lose a lot of weight. As soon as they're together, however, they start indulging again. Sam and Diane in an effort to convince them that this is foolish, take Woody and Beth out to dinner. Hearing the strength of their words, the couple depart, leaving Sam and Diane alone at the table, eating everything that *they* can.

C. Episode Seventy Five

"Someday My Prince Will Come"

Written by Tom Seeley and Norm Gunzenhauser; Directed by James Burrows

Guest Starring: Frank Dent (Stuart)

When Diane finds a Cashmere coat left behind at Cheers, she starts wondering about who the owner is and fantasizes that this could be the man of her dreams; the one she has waited years to find. After listening to this for quite some time, Sam insists that if the man comes back for the coat, Diane will have to go out with him on a date. Eventually the man, Stuart, calls Cheers and Diane speaks to him. They arrange a blind date and when he arrives at the bar to pick her and the coat up, Diane is pleasantly surprised to find him to be an intellectual with quite a bit of money and a good position at his company. Unfortunately, he is far from the best looking guy on the face of the Earth and Diane backs out of the date. She is angry at herself for allowing looks to be such an important issue.

D. Episode Seventy One

"The Groom Wore Clearasil"

Written by Peter Casey and David Lee; Directed by James Burrows

Guest Starring: Timothy Williams (Anthony Tortelli), Mandy Ingber (Annie)

Carla's 16 year old son Anthony tells her that he wants to marry his high school sweetheart, Annie. Carla is stunned and against the whole idea, fearful that Anthony will make the same mistake that she did by getting married at such a young age. She turns to Sam and asks him to talk to her son. Although not crazy about the idea of getting involved, he does so as a favor to Carla. Apparently his words have an effect.

E. Episode Seventy Eight

"Diane's Nightmare"

Written by David Lloyd; Directed by James Burrows

Guest Starring: Derek McGrath (Andy Shroeder)

Diane's old "friend" Andy Schroeder is back in town, or at least that's what she's heard and she is petrified. Her fear becomes out and out paranoia that he will get her. Then she awakens from what turns out to be a dream. Later, at Cheers, Frasier tells her that he has been treating Andy and that the man is making a remarkable recovery. Shortly thereafter, Diane is horrified to see Andy walk in with is new girlfriend and everyone at Cheers treats him like their best friend. At that moment, she awakens from this dream within a dream.

F. Episode Seventy Three

"I'll Gladly Pay You Tuesday"

Written by Cheri Eichen and Bill Steinkellner; Directed by James Burrows

Guest Starring: William Lanteau (Mr. Sayers)

After loaning Diane $500 so she can buy a rare first edition of a Hemingway novel, Sam starts to get concerned that he'll never get paid back. To allay his fears, Diane gives him the book itself as collateral. Trying to get a handle on what's so great about Hemingway, Sam starts to read the book in the tub and accidentally drops it in the water. Sam manages to avoid the issue for several days, but then a collector offers Diane $1,000 for the book, and she asks Sam to give it back to her. Claiming that he can't let her part with such a treasure, he offers to buy it for an additional $500, thus equaling the collector's offer. Touched by his sudden interest in literature, she agrees. At the same time, Diane finds herself very attracted to Sam until she learns the truth.

G. Episode Seventy Four

"2 Good 2 Be 4 Real"

Written by Peter Casey and David Lee; Directed by James Burrows

Guest Starring: Don Lewis (Scotto, the mime)

Feeling that working at Cheers is preventing her from meeting the marrying kind of guy, Carla takes out a personal ad in the local paper. Days pass and she doesn't get any response, which causes her to slip further into depression. Sam comes up with the idea of creating a man for her. Essentially they will respond to her ad and hopefully boost her spirits. This is done and Carla becomes extremely excited, going to the point of turning down flesh and blood men who do respond. Finally Sam is forced to tell her the truth and a furious Carla accepts a date with someone who came to meet her at Cheers: a mortician. While this is going on, Diane tries to help a mime get a "gig" at Cheers. Despite Sam's opposition, he performs and the bar starts *losing* business.

H. Episode Seventy Six

"Love Thy Neighbor"

Written by David Angell; Directed by James Burrows

Guest Starring: Miriam Flynn (Phyllis)

Much of Norm Peterson's time at Cheers is spent verbally abusing his never seen wife, Vera. And if he's not abusing her, then he's making light of the fact that he spends all of his non-work time at Cheers rather than at home. In "Love Thy Neighbor," however, he is forced to examine his true feelings for the woman when Phyllis, a woman who lives next door, comes to him with the feeling that her husband is having an affair with Vera. Not in his wildest imagination can Norm imagine Vera going after another man, but to placate Phyllis he agrees to bring in a private investigator. While they're waiting for a response, Norm and Phyllis convince themselves that their respective spouses are indeed carrying on with each other, and this moves them to almost have an affair themselves. Then the P.I. shows up and informs the duo that there is *nothing* going on between them. A little disappointed over this revelation because it prevents them from carrying on an affair of their own, Norm and Phyllis settle back in to their normal routines. One difference, however, is that Norm leaves Cheers a little earlier than usual to go home and see his wife.

I. Episode Seventy Nine

"From Beer to Eternity"

Written by Peter Casey and David Lee; Directed by James Burrows

Guest Starring: John Calvin (Gary)

In one of the many battles with Gary's Old Time Tavern, the Cheers gangs take on another challenge to see which bar is better. This time they're involved in a bowling match, and Sam is distraught over the fact that his team stinks. The only great player among them is Woody, who refuses to play because he once maimed someone during a similar "tournament." Cheer's only saving grace, of all people, is Diane, who helps bring them to victory, although she threatens bodily harm to the first who tells anyone that she is able to bowl.

J. Episode Seventy Seven

"The Bar Stoolie"

Written by Andy Cowan and Dave Williger; Directed by James Burrows

Guest Starring: Dick O'Neill (Mr. Clavin), Claudia Cron (Claudia)

Sam has been dating Claudia, who is something of an intellectual and that's why he's done his best to make sure that Diane hasn't met her. Eventually they do meet and the two women get along famously. So well, in fact, that Claudia asks Diane to join them on one of their dates. During that evening, Diane's comments about Sam causes Claudia to realize that there's nothing more to the man beyond his looks, and she dumps him. Meanwhile, a concurrent storyline concerns Cliff's reunion with his father, who he hasn't seen since he was a child. Cliff is nervous but is thrilled to learn that the two of them are quite similar in their personalities. His joy turns to shock, however, when he discovers that the man is wanted by the police for a real estate scam he was involved in. This is a one-time only reunion for them.

K. Episode Eighty

"Don Juan is Hell"

Written by Phoef Sutton; Directed by James Burrows

Guest Starring: Kenneth Tigar (Dr. Lowell Greenspon)

Diane asks Sam if it would be okay to use him as the subject of her psychology term paper. Ego instantly swelling, he agrees. The result is a paper on the "Don Juan Syndrome." Sam forgets about the whole thing, until Diane's instructor and fellow classmates come down to Cheers to see the subject of her paper for themselves. It turns out that the "Don Juan Syndrome" has to do with a man who is unable to make a commitment to anyone; who is out for sex only and doesn't have the maturity to handle a non-sexual relationship. Sam is hurt by this, but Diane tries to use their non-sexual friendship as an example. Deep down, of course, they realize that this isn't true at all. Their relationship, even if they keep it hidden, is extremely sexual.

L. Episode Eighty One

"Fools and Their Money"

Written by Heide Perlman; Directed by James Burrows

Despite the fact that he's been winning, everyone at Cheers grows concerned over Woody's obsession with betting on football games. Deciding that he wants to utilize his life savings on a major game, he turns to Sam for assistance to make sure he doesn't screw anything up. Sam, worried that Woody could lose everything he has, doesn't place the bet and is horrified when he

learns that Woody would have won. Now he has to break the news to him. Sam does so, and is stunned when Woody hugs him in response. It seems that Woody feels his action was the nicest thing that anyone has ever done for him. Who can ever figure the Woodman out?

M. Episode Eighty Six

"Take My Shirt....Please?"

Written by David Lloyd; Directed by James Burrows

Guest Starring: Robert Symonds (Mr. Brubaker), Frances Bay (Mrs. Brubaker)

While Norm tries to boost his business by socializing with potential clients who have absolutely nothing in common with him, Sam donates his old baseball jersey to a celebrity auction. This leads Sam to reminisce about his days of fame, only to discover that no one remembers him when there are no bids on the shirt.

N. Episode Eighty Two

"Suspicion"

Written by Tom Reeder; Directed by James Burrows

When a man sits at the bar observing everything going on, writing down notes and speaking into a tape recorder, the group begins to wonder what's going on. When their curiosity becomes genuine concern, Diane has to step forward and admit that the man is a member of her psychology class who has come to Cheers to watch the regulars in action, make observations and report on them to the class. The man's studies are called off, with Sam and the others vowing to get revenge on Diane for allowing them to be used in such a way. Days pass and nothing happens, with Diane talking only about their childish attitudes toward revenge. Basically they ignore her, not doing anything. Then a local television station sends a crew to Cheers to video tape Diane as one of the city's new wave of poets. Diane, of course, thinks it's all a big joke planned by the others, so instead of reading poetry she impersonates a chicken, only to learn the horrifying truth that the news crew was real. Not only is she depressed over making such a spectacle of herself, but she's down because the Cheers gang doesn't care enough about her to get even. This turns out to be a false fear, too, as she enters Sam's office to receive a bucket of water on her head.

O. Episode Eighty Three

"The Triangle"

Written by Susan Seeger; Directed by James Burrows

Diane enlists Sam's reluctant assistance in helping restore Frasier's competence. He has been out of sorts ever since Diane broke up with him in Europe.

P. Episode Eighty Five

"Cliffie's Big Score"

Written by Heide Perlman; Directed by James Burrows

The annual Postman's Ball is, as ever, the highlight of Cliff's social calendar. This year he even has a date. In fact, he has two dates, which poses a bit of a dilemma compounded by the fact that the two women are Carla and Diane. Cliff turns to Sam for help in resolving this unfortunate mess without losing his head.

Q. Episode Eighty Four

"Second Time Around"

Written by Cheri Eichen and Bill Steinkellner; Directed by James Burrows

Guest Starring: Jennifer Tilly (Candi Pearson), Bebe Neuwirth (Dr. Lilith Sternin)

Sam's efforts to help Frasier out of his depression have surprising results: Sam gets Frasier with Candi, hoping to provide Frasier with a good, wild time—only to have Frasier announce his plans to marry the party girl!

R. Episode Eighty Seven

"The Peterson Principle"

Written by Peter Casey and David Lee; Directed by James Burrows

Guest Starring: Chip Zien (Jeff Robbins), Daniel Davis (Mr. Reinhardt)

Norm's ethics are in an uproar: he and a co-worker are up for a major promotion when Norm hears a piece of gossip that could stall the other man's career and advance his own. As Norm faces this moral dilemma, Frasier shows Diane slides of their big European trip, hoping to rekindle the flame of their defunct romance.

S. Episode Eighty Eight

"Dark Imaginings"

Written by David Angell; Directed by James Burrows

Guest Starring: Pamela Bach (Bonnie)

Sam begins to worry that he's getting old when a series of events, such as a date with a younger woman and an embarrassing racketball game with Woody, leave him questioning his vigor.

T. Episode Eighty Nine

"Save the Last Dance For Me"

Written Heide Perlman; Directed by James Burrows

Guest Starring: Dan Hedaya (Nick Tortelli), Jean Kasem (Loretta Tortelli)

Carla enters a dance contest— with her obnoxious ex-husband Nick as her partner! This just doesn't work out, so Carla teams with Sam, and Nick teams with his new bride. While this is a (relatively) more harmonious situation, Carla and Nick realize that they can only win the contest with each other, and leave Sam and Loretta in the lurch.

U. Episode Ninety

"Fear is My Co-Pilot"

Written by Cheri Eichen and Bill Steinkellner; Directed by James Burrows

Guest Starring: Jack Dalton (Pilot)

Jack Dalton, a wild-and-wooly pilot, invites Sam and Diane for a ride in his small plane— only to collapse, unconscious, once they're airborne. The panic-stricken pair reveal their true feelings for each other, but retreat once the crisis is passed.

V. Episode Ninety One

"Diane Chambers Day"

Written by Kimberly Hill; Directed by James Burrows

Frasier arranges to lift Diane out of depression; she feels that she's an outsider at the bar, and so Frasier enlists everyone's aid to make her feel a part of the scene. Diane is overwhelmed by this show of camaraderie (which isn't too easy for some— particularly Carla), but mistakenly believes that it was Sam's idea, and she begins to feel her old feelings for him once again.

W. Episode Ninety Five

"Relief Bartender"

Written by Miriam Trogdon; Directed by James Burrows

Guest Starring: Tony Carrierro (Ken)

A new bartender with a smooth style wins over all the Cheers customers, leaving Woody feeling like a clumsy oaf. His efforts to show up his rival all backfire, and he begins to fear that Sam is going to can him.

X. Episode Ninety Two

"Strange Bedfellows—Part I"

Written by David Angell; Directed by James Burrows

Guest Starring: Kate Mulgrew (Janet Eldridge)

Sam's current romantic interest, Janet Eldridge, runs for city council, and Sam leaps at the opportunity to help her campaign. As the relationship grows more serious, Diane decides to support Janet's competitor, hoping that if Janet loses the race she will also lose Sam, leaving him to Diane.

Y. Episode Ninety Three

"Strange Bedfellows—Part II"

Written by David Angell; Directed by James Burrows

Guest Starring: Kate Mulgrew (Janet Eldridge), Gary Hart (Himself)

Janet convinces Sam to make a clean break with his past— primarily by firing Diane! But Diane quits before Sam can carry out this plan of action. Meanwhile, Norm is squirming under the ceaseless sexual advances of his sister-in-law.

Z. Episode Ninety Four

"Strange Bedfellows—Part III"

Written by David Angell; Directed by James Burrows

Guest Starring: Kate Mulgrew (Janet Eldridge)

Diane poses as a reporter at a press conference for the newly-elected council member Janet Eldridge, where she harasses Sam until he loses his temper and forcibly ejects her. Janet demands that Sam get serious and make a commitment— marriage! The episode ends with Sam proposing marriage over the phone— but who is he proposing to, Janet or Diane?

SEASON FIVE

(1986-1987)

Ted Danson, Kirstie Alley and Roger Rees

A. Episode Ninety Six

"The Proposal"

Written by Peter Casey and David Lee; Directed by James Burrows

The mystery of Sam's proposal is resolved, as he prepares to spend the evening with the woman he plans to marry— Diane Chambers.

B. Episode Ninety Eight

"The Cape Cad"

Written by Andy Cowan and David Williger; Directed by James Burrows

Diane decides that she wants to settle down with Sam, but he's changed his mind about commitment and is chasing every woman who catches his eye. When Diane refuses to believe that he wants to live that way, he goes to extreme lengths to convince her that he's having the time of his life.

C. Episode Ninety Seven

"Money Dearest"

Written by Janet Leahy; Directed by James Burrows

Guest Starring: Frances Sternhagen (Ester Clavin), Paul Wilson (Duncan Fitzgerald)

Cliff is happy when his mother gets involved with a rich man that he introduced her to— until wedding bells seem imminent.

D. Episode One Hundred and Two

"Abnormal Psychology"

Written by Janet Leahy; Directed by James Burrows

Guest cast: Bebe Neuwirth (Dr. Lilith Sternin)

Bebe Neuwirth makes her *Cheers* debut in this episode. Frasier lands a slot on a TV-show debate between respected psychiatrists learns that his opponent is the formidable Dr. Lilith Sternin, a.k.a. "Dr. Sigmund Frost." It seems that Frasier once dated her; his apprehension convinces Diane that he really has strong feelings for Lilith, and so Diane decides to play Cupid, with wacky results.

E. Episode One Hundred

"House of Horrors With Formal Dining and Used Brick"

Written by David Angell; Directed by James Burrows

Carla buys a house, and discovers undreamed-of aspects of Cliff's personality when he stays over to help her cope with what she believes to be a supernatural infestation.

F. Episode Ninety Nine

"Tan N' Wash"

Written by Cheri Eichen and Bill Steinkellner; Directed by James Burrows

Things get hot for Norm when he talks the Cheers gang into investing in his combination laundromat/tanning salon— and the business goes belly-up.

G. Episode One Hundred and Six

"Young Dr. Weinstein"

Written by Phoef Sutton; Directed by James Burrows

Diane can't keep quiet about her impending date at an expensive, upscale restaurant, so Sam cancels her reservations and poses as a renowned surgeon to get his own reservations. Diane is shattered when she can't get in. She sees Sam inside and plots a suitable revenge.

H. Episode One Hundred and Three

"Knights of the Scimitar"

Written by Jeff Abugov; Directed by James Burrows

Guest Starring: J. Eddie Peck (Lance Apollonaire)

Norm's really not interested in joining Cliff's lodge, The Knights of Scimitar, but does when he's convinced that it will help his business. All goes smoothly, until he finds out what the rules are. Meanwhile, Diane uses a college student who likes her in order to make Sam jealous.

I. Episode One Hundred and Seven

"Thanksgiving Orphans"

Written by Cheri Eichen and Bill Steinkellner; Directed by James Burrows

Diane's plans for Thanksgiving are exclusive, so the rest of the gang winds up spending the evening at Carla's. The preparations for dinner go on and on. Diane shows up, having been embarrassed at the other party— but Carla still hasn't put any food on the table! Once dinner is finally served, everyone's frustration gives way in a food fight of epic proportions.

J. Episode One Hundred and Eight

"Everyone Imitates Art"

Written by Heide Perlman; Directed by James Burrows

Diane submits a poem to a literary review and is crushed when all she receives is a letter of rejection. She feels even worse when the magazine publishes a poem submitted by Sam— now she's convinced that she'll never be a writer. But she feels much better when she learns that Sam didn't actually write the poem in question!

K. Episode One Hundred and One

"The Book of Samuel"

Written by Phoef Sutton; Directed by James Burrows

Guest Starring: Amanda Wyss (Beth Curtis), John Brace (Leonard Twilley), Katherine McGrath (Desiree Harrison), Raye Birk (Walt Twitchell)

Sam goes fishing and leaves Woody in charge. Woody is upset to learn that his home-town girlfriend, Beth, is engaged to his old rival Leonard Twilley. Things heat up when the couple decides to visit Woody en route to Niagara Falls. Diane suggests that Woody invent an imaginary girlfriend, but Beth and Leonard confuse matters by asking to meet her. Woody turns to Sam's little black book, and calls Disiree, who Sam has given a five-star rating! Desiree turns out to be Sam's cleaning woman, the stars being a tribute to her professional skills, but she and Woody hit it off anyway, and plan to see each other again.

L. Episode One Hundred and Ten

"Dance, Diane, Dance"

Written by Jeff Abugov; Directed by James Burrows

Guest Starring: Marilyn Lightstone (Madame Likova), Dan Gerrity (Choreographer)

Diane is at home when her dance instructor stops by the bar and everyone learns just what a terrible dancer Diane really is. But since they believe that she'll never dance again, the gang tells Diane that the teacher had nothing but high praise for her!

Cliff's old Chevy won't run, so he buys a Alfa Romeo and foists his old car off on Woody. But the sporty import turns out to be the real lemon, and all Woody has to do to get the Chevy moving is to release the hand brake. Meanwhile, Diane almost tries out for a major ballet company, but is saved from humiliation in the nick of time by Frasier.

M. Episode One Hundred and Eleven

"Chambers Vs. Malone"

Written by David Angell; Directed by James Burrows

Guest Starring: Tom Babson (Himself), Tom Troupe (Judge Grey), Michael Keys Hall (Delaney)

Diane arrives at work with a feeling that Sam is about to propose to her. When a Cheers customer has another hunch which proves correct, the superstitious Carla is convinced that today is a day when all such premonitions are valid, and warns Sam to be careful. But later, in private, Sam tells Diane that he will never propose again. When she begins to cry, he caves in and proposes after all; Diane refuses, since he's only proposing because she's manipulated him into it. Sam loses his temper and pursues Diane out into the street. When Diane falls and injures herself as a result of Sam's irate pursuit, she presses assault charges against him! A Cheers customer agrees to act as Sam's counsel, and arranges a unique plea-bargain: Diane will drop all her charges against Sam if he proposes to her one more time. This time, Diane accepts, and she

and Sam are, at last, officially engaged.

N. Episode One Hundred and Twelve

"Diamond Sam"

Written by Tom Reeder; Directed by James Burrows

Guest Starring: Al Rosen (The Man Who Said Sinatra)

When Diane and Sam officially announce their engagement to the gang, Norm decides to help Sam get an "affordable" engagement ring while Carla tries to convince herself that it isn't true. Sam buys a cheap copy of the ring Diane wants, but she is suspicious and he must go through a complicated series of deceptions. Ultimately, he gives up and buys the first ring after all. But Diane thinks that the ring is fake and throws it out of the car window. Sam and Diane search all night until they find it.

When Carla finally faces the truth that Sam is going to marry Diane, she lets loose with a bloodcurdling cry that nearly traumatizes everyone in the bar.

O. Episode One Hundred and Nine

"Spellbound"

Written by Kimberly Hill; Directed by James Burrows

Guest Starring: Jean Kasem (Loretta Tortelli), Dan Hedaya (Nick Tortelli)

Loretta Tortelli turns to Carla, of all people, for help when she discovers that Nick is cheating on her. Diane and Carla comfort Laura and convince her not to go back to Nick right away. Sam gets involved too, causing Nick to think that Sam is trying to win Loretta; Nick vows to get Diane away from Sam! Instead, he wins Diane's support in getting his wife back. But Loretta is not placated when she discovers Nick kissing Carla!

P. Episode One Hundred and Four

"Never Love a Goalie—Part I"

Written by Ken Levine and David Isaacs; Directed by James Burrows

Guest Starring: Jay Thomas (Eddie LeBec), Doris Grau (Corinne), Hugh Maguire (Hugh), Brent Spiner (Bill Grand), Suzanne Collins (Sherry Grand)

Diane serves on a jury— and can't wait to spill the details of the case to the gang at Cheers. Meanwhile, Carla meets Eddie LeBec, a new goalie for the Bruins who has turned the teams around with five straight wins. When Eddie gives Carla tickets, Frasier decides to go to a game— to "study" the psychology of hockey and its followers. When the inquisitive psychiatrist winds up in jail after a fight at the game, he claims to have really enjoyed the altercation! When Eddie starts dating Carla, he begins to lose his edge, and the Bruins lose again.

Q. Episode One Hundred and Five

"Never Love a Goalie—Part II"

Written by Ken Levine and David Isaacs; Directed by James Burrows

Guest Starring: Jay Thomas (Eddie LeBec), William B. Jackson (Male Juror #1), Laura Waterbury (Female Juror #1), Linda Hoy (Female Juror #2), James Hawthorne (Male Juror #2), John Fleck (Bailiff), Brent Spiner (Bill Grand), Suzanne Collins (Sherry Grand)

The Carla/Eddie romance has a problem: Carla seems to be a jinx. Eddie's game is absolutely no good at all since they started dating. Carla refuses to believe that she has any effect on Eddie's playing, and tries to prove it— by dumping him right before a game! But without Carla, Eddie plays like a genius, and Carla must face the truth. At last, a solution is worked out: they'll date, but she'll dump him before every game and get back together with him afterwards. Amazingly, this convoluted scheme works.

Meanwhile, Diane is the sole juror who believes that the defendant in her case, Bill Grand (Brent Spiner, on the verge of *Star Trek: The Next Generation*), is guilty of attempted murder. She's disappointed when Grand's wife drops all charges, but seizes the opportunity to implement some justice when the reconciled couple comes into the bar for a couple of drinks!

R. Episode One Hundred and Fifteen

"One Last Fling"

Written by Cheri Eichen and Bill Steinkellner; Directed by James Burrows

Guest Starring: Peter Schreiner (Pete), Alan Koss (Alan), Steve Giannelli (Steve), Mark Arnott (Mark), Hugh McGuire (Hugh), Tim Cunningham (Tim), Larry Harpel (Larry)

Diane infiltrates Sam's bachelor party by arranging to be the woman who pops out of the obligatory cake. But while inside the cake, she hears him express regret about his decision to spend the rest of his life with only one woman. She offers Sam a compromise: they will each have twenty-four hours to indulge their every urge with other people.

Sam spends his night spying on Diane from a tree outside her apartment—

Diane spends her night taking pictures of Sam in the tree. With five minutes left in their arrangement, they fall into each others' arms.

S. Episode One Hundred and Thirteen

"Dog Bites Cliff"

Written by Joanne Pagliaro; Directed by James Burrows

Guest Starring: Anita Morris (Madeline Keith)

While Diane is away visiting a Buddhist monastery, Cliffs is bitten by a dog, and plans to sue the dog's owner until he discovers that the owner is a gorgeous, sexy woman named Madeline. Madeline seems to fall for Cliff; the others try to tell him that she's just playing up to him in order to make him drop the lawsuit. He is convinced by her love and is so carried away by passion that he signs a paper without looking at it. Medeline immediately dumps him, but Cliff still believes that she loves him. The gang at the bar pretend to feel sorry for his ridiculous situation.

T. Episode One Hundred and Fourteen

"Dinner at Eight-ish"

Written by Phoef Sutton; Directed by James Burrows

Guest Starring: Zetta Whitlow (Jill), Hugh McGuire (Hugh), Al Rosen (Man Who Said Sinatra)

When Sam and Diane discover that Frasier has asked Dr. Lilith Sternin to live with him, they arrange to have dinner together with the new couple. When Sam and Diane arrive at the Crane residence they sense tension; Frasier was late, and Lilith is angry.

Her mood does not improve when she learns of Frasier's former relationship with Diane. After examining matters from a psychological perspective, it is concluded that the Frasier/Diane relationship is dead, and peace is restored— until the young woman helping Lilith in the kitchen turns out to be one of Sam's old girlfriends!

Meanwhile, Cliff has a rough night when he agrees to babysit for Carla.

U. Episode One Hundred and Seventeen

"Simon Says"

Written by Peter Casey and David Lee; Directed by James Burrows

Guest Starring: John Cleese (Dr. Simon Finch-Royce), Ray Underwood (Busman)

Monty Python's John Cleese guest stars in this episode. Fittingly, Cleese was also the star of Britain's *Fawlty Towers* series, one of the inspirations for *Cheers*. Here, Cleese portrays Dr. Simon Finch-Royce, an internationally famous marriage counsellor, who stops in at Cheers for a drink with his friend Frasier Crane. Diane talks the doctor into a short session with her and Sam; Fich-Royce declares that they are the worst-matched couple he's ever seen. It's a good thing that he told them in time to save them a lifetime of suffering. Diane cannot accept this pronouncement, and proceeds to make Dr. Finch-Royce's life a living hell by dragging Sam to the doctor's hotel room for session after session. Finally, in exasperation, Dr. Finch-Royce reverses his verdict and pronounces Sam and Diane to be the most perfectly suited couple he's ever met.

V. Episode One Hundred and Sixteen

"The Godfather Part III"

Written by Chris Cluess and Stuart Kreisman; Directed by James Burrows

Guest Starring: Al Rosen (Man Who Said Sinatra), Cady McClain (Joyce), Joe Coligan (Jack)

Sam's goddaughter Joyce comes to Boston, and a concerned Sam arranges to have Woody be her escort around town— only to have the two of them announce their plans to live together. Sam and Diane frantically try to talk them out of it.

W. Episode One Hundred and Eighteen

"Norm's First Hurrah"

Written by Andy Cowan and David S. Williger; Directed by Thomas Lofardd

Diane tries to help Norm become a more efficient, gung-ho executive. He's not so keen on the idea, and is embarrassed when his new job with a leading CPA firm doesn't turn out to be what he or his friends expected.

X. Episode One Hundred and Nineteen

"Cheers: The Motion Picture"

Written by Phoef Sutton; Directed by Tim Berry

Guest Starring: Doris Grau (Corinne), Al Rosen (Man Who Said Sinatra)

The Cheers regulars team up to make a home movie designed to convince Woody's Indiana parents that Boston is not the violent, crime-ridden city they believe it to be. However, Diane's intellectual approach to the filmmaking process throws a few kinks into the procedures.

Y. Episode One Hundred and Twenty

"A House is Not a Home"

Written by Phoef Sutton; Directed by Tim Berry

Guest Starring: Douglas Seale (Bert Miller), Billie Bird (Lillian Miller)

The soon-to-be wed Sam and Diane find a house to purchase. Diane is moved when the elderly couple who are moving out share their memories of forty years together in that home and she arranges for them to be able to celebrate one last Christmas celebration there.

Z. Episode One Hundred and Twenty One

"I Do, Adieu"

Written by Glen and Les Charles; Directed by James Burrows

Shelley Long takes a bow as intellectual barmaid Diane Chambers, in the conclusion of her hot-and-cold running romance with Sam Malone. In the end, Diane backs out of the marriage and decides to go off and write a novel, leaving a bewildered Sam in the lurch.

Ted Danson
as Sam Malone

SEASON SIX

(1986-1987)

Kelsey Grammer and John Ratzenberger

A. Episode One Hundred and Twenty Two

"Home is the Sailor"

Written by Glen and Les Charles; Directed by James Burrows

Guest Starring: Jonathan Stark (Wayne), Al Rosen (Man Who Said Sinatra)

A lot has changed since Diane Chambers ditched Sam Malone; Sam sold the bar and sailed off around the world, hoping to ease his woes. Most of the gang doesn't visit Cheers anymore, except Frasier, who finds it less interesting than it was in the old days. Suddenly, Sam shows up: his boat sank, leaving him with no possessions. When he sets eyes on Rebecca Howe (Kirstie Alley), the bar's new manager, he decides to get his old job back. Again, sexual tension is obvious, but now it's a power struggle as well— and Sam is *not* in charge. With this ripe situation in place, its no surprise when Cliff and Norm show up to watch the pyrotechnics!

B. Episode One Hundred and Twenty Five

"'I' On Sports'"

Written by Ken Levine and David Isaacs; Directed by James Burrows

Guest Starring: Fred Dryer (Dave Richards), Catherine MacNeal (Joanne)

Hunter star Fred Dryer, one of the actors originally considered for the role of Sam Malone, guest stars as Sam's sportcaster friend, Dave Richards. Richards talks Sam into taking his spot on the nightly newscast while Richards is on vacation. But Sam can't get the night off so he lies to Rebecca, claiming that his apartment was robbed! The gang, eager to see Sam's television debut, try to keep it a secret from Rebecca, but she learns the truth.

After Sam's first night as a sportscaster goes well, the main anchorperson, Joanne, urges him to spice up his presentation. Unfortunately, this goes to Sam's head, and he tries some absurd techniques to enliven the proceedings— much to his friends' embarrassment, and Rebecca's amusement. If rapping the sports wasn't bad enough, doing it (badly) with a ventriloquist's dummy is the last straw, and Sam is fired from the TV station.

C. Episode One Hundred and Twenty Six

"Little Carla, Happy At Last—Part I"

Written by Cheri Eichen and Bill Steinkellner; Directed by James Burrows

Guest Starring: Jay Thomas (Eddie LeBec), Timothy Williams (Anthony Tortelli), Mandy Ingber (Annie Tortelli), Janet Brandt (Mama LeBec)

Eddie LeBec proposes marriage to Carla, countless kids and all, even when he finds out that she is pregnant again— with twins! But Carla and Eddie are both extremely superstitious, and have some difficulty planning the proper day and time for the wedding. Things take a turn for the worst when Eddie's mother shows up, despises Carla, and talks her son out of the marriage.

D. Episode One Hundred and Twenty Seven

"Little Carla, Happy At Last—Part II"

Written by Cheri Eichen and Bill Steinkellner; Directed by James Burrows

Guest Starring: Jay Thomas (Eddie Le-Bec), Timothy Williams (Anthony Tortelli), Mandy Ingber (Annie Tortelli), Janet Brandt (Mama LeBec), Ed Williams (Father Barry), Ron Husmann (Bandleader)

Sam throws all his weight into getting Carla and Eddie back together again, but it's no simple task. Getting them to the church on time is the least of his problems. But ultimately, Carla becomes Mrs. Eddie LeBec— even though she and her equally superstitious new husband are convinced that the marriage is marked for disaster. Sure enough, the Carla jinx hits again when Eddie is dropped by his hockey team for being too old, and Carla has to return to Cheers to support her family, which now includes not only her unemployed husband, but her son Anthony and *his* wife Annie.

E. Episode One Hundred and Twenty Three

"The Crane Mutiny"

Written by David Angell; Directed by James Burrows

The Cheers gang pull a prank on Frasier when they convince him that Rebecca Howe is in love with him. He breaks off with Lilith by leaving her a letter, only to discover that he's been duped. Lilith is furious, and teams up with Rebecca to get even— only to have Frasier propose to her.

F. Episode One Hundred and Twenty Eight

"Paint Your Office"

Written by Peter Casey and David Lee; Directed by James Burrows

Norm faces a crisis: with a nine hundred dollar tab at Cheers, he can no longer charge his drinks! Tragedy is averted, however, when Rebecca allows Norm to pay off his bar bill by repainting her office. In the process, Norm makes an amazing discovery: Rebecca Howe is actually a very nice person. Pleased with his work, she arranges to have him paint her home as well.

Needless to say, Sam is not terribly interested in Norm's insights into the "real" Rebecca Howe. . . he just wants to "help" Norm paint so he can try to get to see another side of Rebecca, too, but not necessarily her personality.

Norm has to leave when a family problem arises, leaving Sam and Rebecca together. Rebecca says something about changing into more comfortable clothes and goes into another room; Sam is convinced that he's about to get lucky, only to have his hopes dashed when Rebecca returns dressed in jogging clothes! The infuriated Rebecca throws Sam out of her house, and tosses out the painting supplies for good measure.

G. Episode One Hundred and Thirty Two

"The Last Angry Mailman"

Written by Ken Levine and David Isaacs; Directed by James Burrows

Guest Starring: Frances Sternhagen (Esther Clavin), Kevin Dunn (Jim McNulty), Don Sparks (Mr. William Cronin)

Cliff Clavin is pleased to learn that his old neighborhood is due to be torn down to make way for a new shopping complex— until he learns that the house he grew up in is also doomed. His mother is also fighting the demolition, until she is offered two hundred fifty thousand dollars for it. Cliff refuses to face the march of progress and stages a protest, chaining himself to a pillar in the middle of the old house. Norm gets him out of this predicament by sawing the pillar in half, and the two barflies barely get out in time as the old structure caves in behind them.

H. Episode One Hundred and Thirty One

"Bidding on the Boys"

Written by David Lloyd; Directed by James Burrows

Guest Starring: Gary Beach (M.C.), Sharon Barr (Connie)

Frasier inadvertently destroys a passionate evening and arouses Lilith's ire when he brings up the subject of a prenuptual agreement. Infuriated, she goes to Cheers, where Rebecca is conducting a charity auction where bachelors are put on the block. Woody and Sam are among the bachelors, and Lilith breaks all records by bidding two thousand dollars for a date with Sam! Sam realizes that Lilith is angry at Frasier, so he helps Frasier follow them on their date. Lilith starts to throw herself at Sam— who wonders if he can withstand temptation long enough for Frasier to come to his rescue. At last, the lovestruck psychiatrist saves the day, and he and Lilith reconcile their differences. Sam, as might be expected, is left with mixed feelings about his "rescue."

I. Episode One Hundred and Twenty Nine

"Pudd'nhead Boyd"

Written Cheri Eichen and Bill Steinkellner; Directed by James Burrows

Guest Starring: Anne Pitoniak (Mary), John Paragon (Grif Palmer)

Passed up for the lead in a local theatre production, Woody is cast as understudy for the role of Mark Twain— and shows up at work every night in full Mark Twain makeup! While in this guise, he befriends an older woman, only to become concerned that she might be falling for "Mark Twain." Sam has a plan to reveal the truth in as painless a fashion as possible— but Woody's new friend saw through his disguise all along, and they remain good friends.

J. Episode One Hundred and Thirty Three

"A Kiss is Still a Kiss"

Written by David Lloyd; Directed by James Burrows

Guest Starring: Tom Skerritt (Evan Drake)

Evan Drake, an executive of the company that owns Cheers, visits the bar and doesn't realize that Rebecca has been yearning for him for several years. When he invites her and a friend to a party, she settles on taking Sam as her date. Sam finds out about her feelings for Drake and advises her to throw caution to the winds, but Drakes response to her passionate declaration leaves her feeling embarrassed, and she leaves the party in a huff. When Drake comes to the bar to tell her he's not angry, Sam convinces Rebecca that Drake *is* still angry, and talks her into pretending that she and Sam are a hot item, in order to appease her boss. Needless to say, she soon discovers Sam's deception, and loses her temper once more.

97

K. Episode One Hundred and Twenty Four

"My Fair Clavin"

Written by Phoef Sutton; Directed by James Burrows

Guest Starring: Karen Akers (Sally)

Cliff Clavin gets a condo and a girlfriend, all in one fell swoop. However, he thinks Sally is too plain so they stay home all the time. Ever helpful, Rebecca sends a beauty magazine home with Cliff, and soon Sally is ready to be unveiled— only to become an instant hit with everyone at the bar. Cliff is none too pleased with this development, but there isn't much he can do about it once it's done.

To keep herself from smoking, Rebecca promises that she'll let Sam have sex with her if he catches her with a cigarette. A game of hide-and-seek ensues, with Rebecca sneaking a puff whenever she can while Sam tries to sneak up on her. Eventually, he succeeds, but gives up his conquest when he realizes that Rebecca absolutely loathes the prospect of sleeping with him. To make matters worse for Sam, he then realizes what his conscience has led him to relinquish: an opportunity to bed his boss!

L. Episode One Hundred and Thirty Six

"Christmas Cheers"

Written by Cheri Eichen and Bill Steinkellner; Directed by James Burrows

Guest Starring: Jayne Modean (Tracy), Al Rosen (Man Who Said Sinatra)

Rebecca insists that everyone work on Christmas Eve, which does little to boost her popularity. To make matters worse, everyone has gotten her a present except Sam. He buys a package of earmuffs from a shopper he meets and gives it to Rebecca— but it turns out to be diamonds instead. Sam is pleasantly surprised when Rebecca invites him to come over to her house, figuring that this gift has won her over, and gladly pays the shopper for the cost of the earrings. But, as might be expected, Sam's libido gets another cold shower when it turns out that *everyone* has been invited to Rebecca's Christmas party!

M. Episode One Hundred and Thirty Four

"Woody For Hire Meets Norman of the Apes"

Written by Phoef Sutton; Directed by James Burrows

Guest Starring: Paddi Edwards (Sylvia), Betty Vaughan (Laura), Robert Urich (Himself)

Woody lands a bit part as an extra on *Spenser: For Hire* and is thrilled to have met Robert Urich. No one believes him because all that can be seen of Woody when the *Spenser* episode is aired is the sleeve of his shirt!

Meanwhile, the friendship between Norm and Cliff is put to the test when Cliff decides not to pay Norm for painting his apartment. Clavin then adds insult to injury by having an orangutan dressed as a painter visit the bar. Sam patches things up between them, but things sour again when Norm pulls the same stunt, but with the ape dressed as a mailman.

A ladie's organization arranges to use the pool room on Sunday nights, but the members drop their genteel façades once their drinks are spiked, alarming Frasier and Sam with their wild behavior.

Finally, Robert Urich comes to the bar, but everyone is busy, and Woody can't get their attention long enough to convince them that he really knows the star.

N. Episode One Hundred and Thirty Five

"And God Created Woodman"

Written by Jeffrey Duteil; Directed by John Ratzenberger

Guest Starring: Peter Hansen (Collier)

Sam and Woody wind up tending bar at a cocktail party that Rebecca has arranged for Daniel Collier, chairman of Cheers' parent company. When Rebecca breaks an expensive vase, Woody takes the blame for her, and the executive is so taken by Woody's honesty that he takes him into his den for drinks, where they become great friends and Collier promises to take Woody skiing.

The following day, a sober Collier barges in, having forgotten about the events of the night before, and demands to know the identity of the person responsible for destroying the vase. Having heard about Woody's good luck, Sam takes the blame this time, and sure enough, he finds himself invited on a skiing trip to Vail, Colorado.

O. Episode One Hundred and Thirty Seven

"A Tale of Two Cuties"

Written by Cheri Eichen and Bill Steinkellner; Directed by Michael Zinberg

Guest Starring: Tom Skerritt (Evan Drake), Timothy Williams (Anthony Tortelli), Mandy Ingber (Annie Tortelli), Bobbies Eakes (Laurie)

Rebecca hires a temporary replacement for Carla when she goes into the hospital to have twins. Rebecca's boss, Evan Drake, suggests an attractive young girl named Laurie. Laurie's casual way of referring to Drake convinces Rebecca that she's just hired Drake's mistress, and Rebecca belts the young woman in the jaw just as Drake enters. Drake reveals that Laurie is his daughter, a fact left unmentioned to avoid preferential treatment for Laurie, who is just entering the workforce. With a little help from Sam, Rebecca manages to convince her boss that the punch was the result of an involuntary nervous disorder.

P. Episode One Hundred and Thirty Eight

"Yacht of Fools"

Written by Phoef Sutton; Directed by Thomas Lofaro

Guest Starring: Tom Skerritt (Evan Drake), Dorothy Parke (Julie), Tom Astor (Lorenzo)

When Evan Drake invites Sam on a weekend yachting expedition, he suggests that Sam bring along Rebecca; he's still convinced that Rebecca and Sam are an item. Sam balks at this idea and invites the gorgeous Julie along instead. But Rebecca forces Sam to pass Julie off as his sister. Rebecca is upset when Drake makes a pass at Julie; Drake feels guilty about hitting on Sam's sister. Drake's remorse restores Rebecca's desire for her boss, but Sam's efforts to land Julie come to naught, as Lorenzo, the steward, has already swept her off her feet.

Q. Episode One Hundred and Thirty Nine

"To All the Girls I've Loved Before"

Written by Ken Levine and David Isaacs; Directed by James Burrows

Frasier's stag party is so much fun he begins to have second thoughts about marrying Lilith. He changes his mind when he learns that she had a bit of fun of her own— with a male stripper at her "bridal shower."

R. Episode One Hundred and Forty

"Let Sleeping Drakes Lie"

Written by David Lloyd; Directed by James Burrows

Guest Starring: Tom Skerritt (Evan Drake), Cec Verrell (Jennifer), Jay Bell (Greyson)

Frasier tells Sam about an extremely beautiful patient of his who is aroused only by men who dance. Sam determines that a beautiful young woman is one of Frasier's patients and tries to win her by pretending to be a dancer. His efforts are in vain, and he can't understand why.

Meanwhile, Norm lands a job painting the interior of Evan Drake's house while Drake is in Europe, and he doesn't have to twist Rebecca's arm when he offers a chance to see her boss' bedroom. She learns more about Drake than she wants to when he returns home early: one, he's a light sleeper, and two, the door of the closet she's hiding in creaks whenever she tries to sneak out. It takes Norm to get Rebecca out of this sticky predicament.

Sam finally discovers the reason that he's been striking out: Frasier has *two* incredibly gorgeous female patients.

One of them is attracted to dancers— but the one that Sam has been going out with is a pyromaniac. . . and she's alone at his apartment!

S. Episode One Hundred and Thirty

"Airport V"

Written by Ken Levine and David Isaacs; Directed by George Wendt

Guest Starring: Jay Thomas (Eddie Le-Bec), Peter Elbling (Murray Treadwell)

Eddie LeBec lands a job at last— he's a skating penguin in an ice show. He flies to Seattle to begin work, but can't get Carla to come with him, as she terrified of going up in a plane. By lucky coincidence, Frasier is conducting a "Fear of Flying" workshop, and manages to calm Carla's fears. In fact, when he and his students test their success by going for a flight, it's Frasier who panics once they're airborne.

In a sideplot, Rebecca goes to dinner with a well-known restaurant critic. When he gives Cheers a good review, everyone thinks that she slept with him.

T. Episode One Hundred and Forty One

"The Sam in the Grey flannel Suit"

Written by Cheri Eichen and Bill Stein-kellner; Directed by Tim Berry

Guest Starring: Tom Skerritt (Evan Drake)

Sam is pleased and Rebecca is depressed when Even Drake makes Mr. Malone a corporate executive. But Drake has an ulterior motive: Sam is really a ringer, designed to assure the company softball team of victory in their league. Rebecca is relieved to learn the truth— but convincing Sam of the truth proves to be another matter entirely.

U. Episode One Hundred and Forty Four

"Our Hourly Bread"

Written by Susan Herring; Directed by Andy Ackerman

Frasier buys Lilith a painting to celebrate their first month of marriage, but she hates it. He donates the painting to a raffle that Sam and Woody are holding to draw new customers to the bar in order to get raises. The winning number is 66— or is it 99? Woody is confused, but matters work out when one of the two winners realizes that the alternative prize is Frasier's painting— a painting that he's always wanted.

V. Episode One Hundred and Forty Three

"Slumber Party Massacred"

Written by Phoef Sutton; Directed by James Burrows

Guest Starring: Jay Thomas (Eddie Le-Bec), Mandy Ingber (Annie), Timothy Williams (Anthony), Elizabeth Ruscio (Dorothy)

The joyous news that she is about to become a grandmother does not sit well with Carla, who instead lapses into a dark, depressed mood. The Cheers women throw a slumber party but she still won't be cheered up, until the guys show up and Cliff rips the seam of his trousers. This spectacle ignites the Tortelli sense of humor, and Carla finally manages to relax and enjoy herself.

W. Episode One Hundred and Forty Seven

"Bar Wars"

Written by Ken Levine and David Isaacs; Directed by James Burrows

Guest Starring: Robert Desiderio (Gary), Wade Boggs (Himself)

Cheers' rival bar, Gary's Old Towne Tavern, gets revenge on Cheers for last years bowling defeat by stealing the bowling trophy and destroying it. A contest (actually a war) of practical jokes erupts between the two establishments. At last Gary admits defeat and arranges for Red Sox player Wade Boggs to go and sign autographs at Cheers. But Sam and the gang think that this is another trick, and de-pants the impostor, who turns out to be the real Boggs after all.

X. Episode One Hundred and Forty Two

"The Big Kiss-Off"

Written by Ken Levine and David Isaacs; Directed by James Burrows

Things get weird at Cheers when Sam and Woody get embroiled in a wager as to which of them can get a kiss from Rebecca before midnight. When Rebecca finds out what's going on, she tricks both men so that they wind up kissing each other in public.

Y. Episode One Hundred and Forty Five

"Backseat Becky, Upfront"

Written by Cheri Eichen and Bill Steinkellner; Directed by James Burrows

Guest Starring: Tom Skerritt (Evan Drake)

The rug is pulled out from under Rebecca's heart when she discovers that her beloved Evan Drake is going to be transferred to the company's Tokyo offices. She tries to reveal her true feelings to Drake but all her attempts to be alone with him fail, and she resigns herself to his departure. Sam gives her a second chance by kidnapping Drake's chauffeur. But when Rebecca starts to tell Drake the truth, he asks her to pick up Christy, the woman who's going to Japan with him. Rebecca crashes the limousine into a convenience store when Drake and Christy start to get intimate in the back of the car and Sam has to bail Rebecca out of prison.

*Kelsey Grammer
as Frasier Crane*

SEASON SEVEN

(1988-1989)

George Wendt and Kirstie Alley

A. Episode One Hundred and Forty Eight

"How to Recede in Business"

Written by David Angell; Directed by James Burrows

Guest Starring: Brian Bedford (Greg Stone)

The season opens with another set of reversals for the Cheers crew. Sam has finally managed to get Rebecca to go out with him. Pans are drastically changed when the company fires Rebecca and gives her old job to Sam.

It doesn't take long for Sam to realize that he can't run things alone, and he talks his boss, Mr. Stone, into rehiring Rebecca. He thinks his kindness will give him leverage to finally get somewhere with Rebecca. Sam and Rebecca reschedual their date, but they encounter Stone, who reveals the one aspect of Rebecca's rehiring that Sam had hoped to keep under wraps, at least long enough to score: she's been rehired as a waitress, with Carla as her boss! Rebecca walks out again, but finally decides to stay at Cheers after all.

B. Episode One Hundred and Forty Six

"Swear to God"

Written by Tom Reeder; Directed by James Burrows

Guest Starring: Eric Christmas (Father Barry), Kim Johnston Ulrich (Rachel)

As usual, Sam can't help flirting with a cute bar customer but stops when his old girlfriend, Chelsea, calls him up and asks to meet. His hopes for this reunion are high until he discovers that Chelsea is pregnant— and that he may be the father. Carla catches Sam praying and cruelly suggests that he atone by giving up something he values— such as sex. Swayed by this suggestion, Sam swears that he'll be celibate for a year.

Meanwhile, Woody is pursuing his career in local theatre. As usual, he's cast as an understudy, but this doesn't stop him from dressing in full costume. When Sam finds out that he's not the father of Chelsea's child, he forgets all about his vow, until he runs into Woody— dressed as Moses, beard, robes and all! Chastened, Sam renews his sacred promise and makes a date with a beautiful woman, one year in the future.

NOTE: This episode was filmed during production of the sixth season but was not aired until the seventh.

C. Episode One Hundred and Forty Nine

"Executive Sweet"

Written by Phoef Sutton; Directed by James Burrows

Guest Starring: Alex Nevil (Martin Teal), Gerald Hiken (Dennis)

Strictly to advance her career, Rebecca dates Martin Teal, a bigwig from the company that owns Cheers. When Sam gives her a hard time about this, she pretends to be wildly in love with Teal, only to have the tables turned on her when Sam arranges for Teal to overhear her "confessions." Rebecca vows to get even with Sam.

D. Episode One Hundred and Fifty Five

"One Happy Chappy in a Snappy Serape"

Written by Cheri Eichen and Bill Steinkellner; Directed by James Burrows

Guest Starring: Alex Nevil (Martin Teal), Gerald Hiken (Dennis), Marco Hernandez (Ramon), Fred Asparagus (Pepe), Nicholas Montealegre (Urchin)

Martin Teal tries to get Rebecca to marry him, but she fends him off by claiming to be engaged to Sam. Sam is all too willing to support this deception, for his own, all too obvious reasons. Teal counters by offering Sam a job at a resort in Mazatlan. With Sam away, Rebecca has nothing but her protestations of her "faith" in Sam to keep Teal away, even when Teal presents evidence that Sam has been playing the field in Mexico. Rebecca flies to Mexico, but nothing will move Sam to return with her, and she finally gives in to Teal's proposal. Sam comes back and interrupts the wedding in the nick of time; the drunken Rebecca offers him a shot at her body, but he can't bring himself to take advantage of her after she passes out.

E. Episode One Hundred and Fifty

"Those Lips, Those Ice"

Written by Peter Casey and David Lee; Directed by James Burrows

Guest Starring: Jay Thomas (Eddie LeBec), Isa Anderson (Franzi Schrempf), Hugh Maguire (Hugh), Alan Koss (Alan), Steve Giannelli (Steve)

Carla thinks that Eddie's cheating on her when his new ice-show skating partner turns out to be the gorgeous East German figure skater Franzi Schrempf. Rather than give into her impulse to kill Eddie, she decides to act out the role of the ideal wife and homemaker. When Franzi's boyfriend turns up, Carla is relieved, and her jealousy serves only to fuel Eddie's love for her.

F. Episode One Hundred and Fifty One

"Norm, Is That You?"

Written by Cheri Eichen and Bill Steinkellner; Directed by James Burrows

Guest Starring: Craig Branham (Todd), B.J. Turner (Ivan), Jane Sibbett (Kim), George Deloy (Robert)

When Norm provides Frasier and Lilith with the decoration touches that their regular interior decorator can't provide, he finds himself touted as a top designer and is offered work by Frasier's trendy friends Robert and Kim. Norm is convinced that he must act the part of an interior decorator in order to keep this newfound job. He plays the part of a gay designer in his dealings with his yuppie clients. All goes well for a while, with Norm free to be his regular self in the bar at nights. But when Robert and Kim come to Cheers and try to set Norm up with their gay friend Michael, he is afraid that he's going to lose the chance to decorate their country home. He chooses to reveal the the truth rather than continue the imposture, and is relieved to discover that the role-playing was unnecessary. His clients value his skills, and it doesn't matter if he's really a beer-swilling slob on his own time.

G. Episode One Hundred and Fifty Eight

"How to Win Friends and Electrocute People"

Written by Phoef Sutton; Directed by James Burrows

Guest Starring: Shirley Prestia (Nurse), Robert Benedetti (Dave), Ed Wright (McManus)

Cliff winds up in the hospital with appendicitis, but is dismayed when none of his friends come to visit him; when Frasier is elected to represent the others, it doesn't help much at all. Cliff decides that his personality is at fault, and decides to use electrical aversion therapy to change his personal habits.

H. Episode One Hundred and Fifty Three

"Jumping Jerks"

Written by Ken Levine and David Isaacs; Directed by James Burrows

Guest Starring: J. Kenneth Campbell (Bob Speakes), Thomas Sanders (Otto)

Woody, Cliff, and Norm go skydiving but lose their nerve, which obliges them to lie about the experience. When Rebecca mentions that skydivers attract her, Sam drags the gang along for another jump— but he can't do it, either. More lies ensue, and Rebecca challenges Sam to repeat his alleged feat, but with a Cheers banner as well. Airborne again, the men try to work up a convincing cover story, but Woody suddenly realizes that he's completely fed up and just jumps. Sam and Norm jump too, banner in tow; Cliff stays on the plane until he learns that it is out of control. The Cheers men finally succeed in skydiving.

I. Episode One Hundred and Fifty Two

"Send in the Crane"

Written by David Lloyd; Directed by James Burrows

Guest Starring: Sandahl Bergman (Judy), Chelsea Noble (Laurie), Brandon Hooper (Tom)

Sam falls for Laurie, the twenty-one year old daughter of his old flame Judy, and contrives to hang out with Judy in order to get closer to her daughter. Meanwhile, Frasier (who's just been given a pair of see-through bikini briefs by Lilith) advises Rebecca to hire Woody to be the clown at a birthday party she's been forced to organize for the child of one of her corporate bosses. When Woody can't do it, Frasier steps in, but he fails utterly until his pants fall, revealing his new underwear.

Sam is about to reveal his true intentions to Judy when Laurie produces her fiance and introduces him to her "uncle." Judy sees through Sam and walks out on him in disgust.

J. Episode One Hundred and Fifty Four

"Bar Wars II: The Woodman Strikes Back"

Written by Ken Levine and David Isaacs; Directed by James Burrows

Guest Starring: Joel Polis (Gary)

Cheers' rivalry with Gary's Old Town Tavern heats up again with the approach of the Boston Bloody Mary Contest, which Gary's bar has won for four years in a row. Using Mata Hari techniques, Rebecca manages to get a sample of Gary's Bloody Mary mix from one of Gary's bartenders, and the gang all try to figure out what's in it. Carla has been looking for a rare ingredient, the spice known as black cardamom, and Sam determines that this is the secret ingredient that they need to beat Gary. But Woody has one allergy: black cardamom. His sneeze wipes out all of the rare substance that Carla could find, and he destroys Gary's Bloody Mary, convinced that it, too, has the irritating spice in it. With nothing to go on, Cheers seems doomed to failure. Everyone turns against Woody, so he quits and goes to work for Gary. This ruse works but he fails to make Gary late for the contest. Woody then poses as a judge but Gary is not fooled by his flimsy disguise, and a real judge declares Gary the winner. After Gary departs, the judge turns out to be Carla's neighbor. Gary will miss the real contest, and Cheers will win the contest after all.

K. Episode One Hundred and Fifty Nine

"Adventures in Housesitting"

Written by Patricia Niedzialek and Cecile Alch; Directed by James Burrows

Guest Starring: Michael Currie (Mr. Sheridan)

Rebecca gets stuck taking care of Buster, the dog of a corporate executive, Sheridan. The dog runs away and Woody produces a similar dog, Satan. Satan is a junkyard guard dog who will attack at the word "Cochise." When Sheridan comes back early, Rebecca must stall until Sam can replace Satan with the real Buster. Finally, Satan winds up at Cheers, where everyone hopes to avoid triggering an attack.

L. Episode One Hundred and Sixty One

"Please Mr. Postman"

Written by Mert Rich and Brian Pollack; Directed by James Burrows

Guest Starring: Annie Golden (Margaret O'Keefe)

Cliff laments his obligation to train a new mail carrier until he learns that she's an attractive woman who shares his obsession with pointless trivia. Even better, Margaret looks up to Cliff, and soon they find themselves being drawn towards each other. A motel tryst goes awry when a cop spots their mail truck outside, but Cliff covers for Margaret, only to break down and admit the truth when his boss confronts him in Cheers. Later, Margaret, not realizing that Cliff gave up her secret, thanks him for protecting her and heads off for a career in the Canadian postal service.

Meanwhile, Sam tries to find out the lyrics to a song that supposedly made Rebecca sexually receptive during her school days— eventually stooping so low as to actually call her mother.

M. Episode One Hundred and Sixty

"Golden Boyd"

Written by Cheri Eichen and Bill Steinkellner; Directed by James Burrows

Guest Starring: Tyrone Power, Jr. (Nash), Jackie Swanson (Kelly Gaines), Richard Doyle (Mr. Gaines)

Rebecca gets Sam and Woody to tend bar at a catered party for Kelly Gaines, the daughter of another company executive. Kelly's obnoxious boyfriend keeps insulting Woody, and they almost come to blows, stopped only by Rebecca's intervention. Meeting in the Cheers pool room the next day, the two men fight, and Woody is beaten. He gets even by dating Kelly, who gets back together with her boyfriend but agrees to see Woody again.

N. Episode One Hundred and Fifty Seven

"I Kid You Not"

Written by Rick Beren; Directed by James Burrows

Guest Starring: Jarrett Lennon (Cody), Jackie Swanson (Kelly)

Carla's six-year-old son Cody, son of a Nobel prize winner, seems to be taking after his father too much, and Carla is determined to turn him into a "real" kid. Things are complicated when Frasier and Lilith "borrow" Cody to learn something about being parents and take him to the opera, which the boy enjoys immensely. Carla decides to get more interested in highbrow pursuits, and joins Frasier, Lilith and Cody at a fancy restaurant.

Woody, meanwhile, undertakes to get the loan of Sam's treasured Corvette for his first serious date with Kelly.

Dinner is very awkward for Carla until Cody acts up and she must calm him down. Her dominion reasserted, she feels much better. Frasier, appalled, decides that having a family is not for him and Lilith. But it's a bit late for such pronouncements, as Lilith is already pregnant.

O. Episode One Hundred and Sixty Two

"Don't Paint Your Chickens"

Written by Ken Levine and David Isaacs; Directed by James Burrows

Guest Starring: Lisa Aliff (Erin), Stefan Gierasch (Mr. Anawalt)

Sam has gotten lucky with a young lady named Erin, but her athletic ways are running him down and making him feel his age. Meanwhile, Rebecca goes to great lengths to bring herself to the attention of her corporate bosses. Eventually, she impresses one big executive, who offers her a huge raise and an executive-level job— just before the FBI arrives to arrest him for tax evasion.

P. Episode One Hundred and Sixty Three

"The Cranemakers"

Written by Phoef Sutton; Directed by James Burrows

Rebecca insists on sending Woody on vacation, as he hasn't had one in four years, and arranges to send him to Italy. Woody's flight is delayed And he misses his flight after falling asleep in the airport.

Frasier and Lilith decide to get away from civilization so they can raise their unborn child in nature. They find that they can't stand nature, and return to the city.

Woody comes back, having had a great time watching and meeting people at the airport terminal. He decides to take time off to hang out at the bus station.

Q. Episode One Hundred and Fifty Six

"Hot Rocks"

Written by Ken Levine and David Isaacs; Directed by James Burrows

Guest Starring: Admiral William J. Crowe (Himself), Al Rosen (Man Who Said Sinatra)

109

Rebecca stays at Cheers after her date to a big social event backs out on her; she's wearing borrowed earrings worth thirty-two thousand dollars. Sam returns from the celebration with the Chairman of the Joint Chiefs of Staff, Admiral Crowe. When Rebecca misplaces the earrings, she thinks that the Admiral stole them, and promises to let Sam sleep with her if he can get them back. Of course the Admiral is not a thief and when Sam finds the missing jewelry, he graciously settles for a kiss instead of the promised sex.

R. Episode One Hundred and Sixty Four

"What's Up Doc?"

Written by Brian Pollack and Mert Rich; Directed by James Burrows

Guest Starring: Madolyn Smith Osborne (Dr. Sheila Rydell)

Sam tries to woo a professional colleague of Frasier's and Lilith's by going to her for professional help— pretending to be suffering from impotence. Although the truth is soon revealed, Dr. Sheila Rydell agrees to go out with Sam. When he pressures her to reveal her psychiatric view of him, he is crushed to learn that he is a shallow man who thinks of nothing unrelated to sex. Rebecca and Sheila have a good laugh but later discover Sam's one non-sexual interest: the Three Stooges.

S. Episode One Hundred and Sixty Five

"The Gift of the Woodi"

Written by Phoef Sutton; Directed by James Burrows

Guest Starring: Jackie Swanson (Kelly)

Cliff invents a plant hybrid, half rutabaga, half beet, but nobody particularly seems to care. Rebecca turns to Lilith for help in dressing for success, but it's Lilith who winds up being offered the position that Rebecca is after. Woody, meanwhile, can't afford an expensive gift for Kelly so he writes a song for her. Kelly fails to understand until he buys her a piece of jewelry which uses up all his life savings; she returns it when he explains the motivation behind the song.

T. Episode One Hundred and Sixty Six

"Call Me Irresponsible"

Written by Dan O'Shannon and Tom Anderson; Directed by James Burrows

Guest Starring: Jay Thomas (Eddie Lebec)

Carla is waiting for Eddie to show up for their second anniversary, only to be crushed when the "present" he sends her turns out to be nothing more than his dirty laundry! The gang send her a bouquet and try to pass it off as being from Eddie, but she isn't taken in for a minute. Carla grows more and more unhappy, until Eddie calls and explains why he couldn't make it.

U. Episode One Hundred and Sixty Eight

"Sisterly Love"

Written by David Lloyd; Directed by James Burrows

Guest Starring: Marcia Cross (Susan Howe), Richmond Harrison (Phil)

When Rebecca's sister, Susan, arrives in Boston to patch up an old falling out, Sam elects himself as peacemaker and sets up dates with both of them on the same night. Susan shows up at the wrong time and involves Sam in a compromising position. Rebecca shows up, pulls a gun, and shoots Susan. A stunned Sam Malone helps Rebecca get rid of the body, only to be caught in the act by all the Cheers regulars. Of course its all been a trick set up by the sisters, who found out about Sam's duplicitous maneuverings and teamed up to embarrass him in a most telling manner.

V. Episode One Hundred and Sixty Seven

"The Visiting Lecher"

Written by David Lloyd; Directed by James Burrows

Guest Starring: John McMartin (Dr. Lawrence Kendall), Fabiana Udenio (Marie Kendall)

Dr. Lawrence Kendall, a respected psychiatrist friend of Frasier, is in Boston. Even though he's a married man, he proceeds to hit on Rebecca. No one will believe her claim so she drags Sam to Kendall's hotel room. But Sam is too preoccupied with a hotel maid to listen much to Rebecca and Kendall's conversation from his vantage point inside Kendall's closet. When Mrs. Kendall shows up, Rebecca confronts her with the truth, but Mrs. Kendall defends her husband and attacks Rebecca, who is dragged away kicking and screaming.

SEASON EIGHT

(1989-1990)

Roger Rees and Kirstie Alley

A. Episode One Hundred and Seventy

"The Improbable Dream—Part One"

Written by Cheri Eichen and Bill Steinkellner; Directed by James Burrows

Guest Starring: Roger Rees (Robin Colcord)

Rebecca has been corresponding with corporate hotshot Robin Colcord but never dreams that she'll meet him. On the other hand, she keeps having erotic dreams in which she succumbs to Sam's seductions. When she asks her psychiatrist friends for help, Sam eavesdrops, and decides to take advantage of her dreams by approaching her while she's napping. An argument gives way to the very real possibility that Sam might get Rebecca at last. This is shattered when the dashing Colcord drops in, erasing all thoughts of Sam from Rebecca's mind.

B. Episode One Hundred and Seventy One

"The Improbable Dream—Part Two"

Written by Cheri Eichen and Bill Steinkellner; Directed by James Burrows

Guest Starring: Roger Rees (Robin Colcord), Al Rosen (Al)

Sam is left in the lurch when Rebecca zooms off to California in Robin Colcord's Lear jet. Her postcards only deepen his sense of being useless, and he keeps having intense dreams about the absent Rebecca. When she comes back, he uses his dream to find out the details of her time with Colcord.

C. Episode One Hundred and Seventy Two

"A Bar is Born"

Written by Phoef Sutton; Directed by James Burrows

Guest Starring: Roger Rees (Robin Colcord)

Sam decides to ditch Cheers and leave his troubles behind by opening his own bar, but Robin Colcord buys the property out and Sam returns to his old job.

D. Episode One Hundred and Seventy Four

"How to Marry a Mailman"

Written by Brian Pollack and Mert Rich; Directed by James Burrows

Guest Starring: Roger Rees (Robin Colcord), Annie Golden (Margaret O'Keefe)

Returning from Canada, Cliff's mail-toting girlfriend, Margaret, tries to rope him into marriage. He's amenable to the idea but is struck blind, which Frasier diagnoses as a paranoid psychosomatic reaction to his fear of commitment. This worked out, and his sight restored, nuptual planning resumes—until Cliff is paralyzed! Margaret leaves to give Cliff time to work out his psychological problems.

E. Episode One Hundred and Seventy Five

"The Two Faces of Norm"

Written by Eugene B. Stein; Directed by Andy Ackerman

Guest Starring: Eric Allen Kramer (Rudy), J.C. Victor (Scott), Mark Knudson (John)

Norm expands his painting business but finds that he can't keep his crew in line, so he creates an alter-ego, the slavedriving Anton Kreitzer. Complications ensue, as his employees pressure him to take a stand against the excesses of his imaginary business partner. Sam, meanwhile, tries to buy back his beloved Corvette (he's bought a Volare instead) when he realizes its importance in maintaining his image.

F. Episode One Hundred and Seventy Three

"The Stork Brings a Crane"

Written by David Lloyd; Directed by Andy Ackerman

Lilith Sternin-Crane prepares to give birth against the backdrop of the bar's one-hundredth anniversary. Sam and Frasier drive her to the hospital, but it turns out that the labor was false. A woman in the next bed over is having a baby with no one at her side, so Sam and Frasier lend her moral support, leaving Lilith to have her son in the cab on her way home.

G. Episode One Hundred and Seventy Seven

"Death Takes a Holiday On Ice"

Written by Ken Levine and David Isaacs; Directed by James Burrows

Guest Starring: Anne DeSalvo (Gloria), Kevin Conroy (Darryl Mead), Eric Christmas (Father Barry)

Eddie is killed in freak accident involving an ice machine, and Carla learns that he was bigamist. She is de-termined to hate his other wife, but the two women meet at the funeral and realize that they would be better off supporting each other through their period of mourning.

H. Episode One Hundred and Seventy Nine

"For Real Men Only"

Written by David Pollock and Elias Davis; Directed by James Burrows

Guest Starring: Jay Robinson (Larry), Michael Currie (Mr. Sheridan), Rick Podell (Dr. Levinson)

In keeping with Lilith's Jewish heritage, she and Frasier plan to hold a bris (the circumcision ritual) for their infant son. Frasier is appalled that the other men are squeamish about witnessing the ceremony, but ultimately panics himself, and takes the baby to Cheers to hide out. Lilith catches up with Frasier and convinces him that its all right, and the ceremony is held in Cheers against the backdrop of a riotous retirement party.

I. Episode One Hundred and Sixty Nine

"Two Girls for Every Boyd"

Written by Dan O'Shannon and Tom Anderson; Directed by James Burrows

Guest Starring: Jackie Swanson (Kelly Gaines), Jeffrey Richman (Lee Bradken), Lisa Kudrow (Emily), Mark Kubr (Torsten)

Woody finally lands a lead in a local production of "Our Town," but can't get the hang of his big love scene. His partner in the scene talks him into practicing in the back room of Cheers. Needless to say, Kelly walks in and then storms out in a huff, leading him to reveal his feelings and break through to new levels of acting prowess.

Meanwhile, Sam, Frasier, and Norm engage Cliff in a beard-growing contest when Cliff insists that the men in his family are particularly good at growing facial hair. Cliff seems to be doomed to lose as time goes by, but true to his genes, a sudden upsurge in hair development pushes him on to triumph.

J. Episode One Hundred and Seventy Six

"The Art of the Steal"

Written by Sue Herring; Directed by James Burrows

While Norm tries to teach Woody a few basic economic concepts by means of a Monopoly game with the guys, Rebecca, armed with a bottle of champagne, goes to Robin Colcord's penthouse apartment. Colcord never shows; instead, Sam shows up with a message and finds a drunk and naked Rebecca. In her anger at this, Rebecca manages to trigger the apartment's alarm system, trapping them there until the maid arrives in the morning.

K. Episode One Hundred and Eighty One

"Feeble Attraction"

Written by Dan O'Shannon and Tom Anderson; Directed by James Burrows

Guest Starring: Roger Rees (Robin Colcord), Cynthia Stevenson (Doris)

Robin Colcord gives Rebecca an old desk and suggests that it conceals a valuable ring. Rebecca is frantic to locate this prize, and eventually cuts the desk in half with a chainsaw, only to learn

that the "ring" in question is the one left on the desk's surface by a wine glass— a wine glass left there by Charles Dickens when he celebrated the conclusion of his "A Tale of Two Cities." Meanwhile, Norm's ex-secretary, obsessed with him, begins to make his life a living hell— until he manages to divert her attention to his pal Cliff.

L. Episode One Hundred and Seventy Eight

"Sam Ahoy"

Written by David Lloyd; Directed by James Burrows

Guest Starring: Roger Rees (Robin Colcord)

Sam's growing desire to buy back Cheers leads him to talk Robin into lending him his boat, "The Rebecca," so that Sam can try for the ten thousand dollar prize in the annual Boston Harbor regatta. With Norm and Carla as his crew, how can he lose? But they place dead last— and almost wind up dead when Norm finds a bomb and a death threat, addressed to Colcord, in the hold of the vessel. They manage to abandon ship before the bomb destroys it. Sam proudly and foolishly refuses to accept any money from Colcord.

M. Episode One Hundred and Eighty Two

"Sammy and the Professor"

Written by Brian Pollack and Mert Rich; Directed by James Burrows

Rebecca's college professor, Professor Volkman, comes into town, and stuns her ex-student by having a fling with Sam! She accuses Sam of taking advantage of the professor but learns that she came on to him. . . and the professor refuses to see anything wrong about the brief affair. Rebecca is thoroughly confused by the situation.

N. Episode One Hundred and Eighty Four

"What is....Cliff Clavin?"

Written by Dan O'Shannon and Tom Anderson; Directed by Andy Ackerman

Guest Starring: Alex Trebec (Himself), Johnny Gilbert (Himself), Greg E. Davis (Timmy)

Cliff Clavin, Cheer's resident master of vast but useless knowledge, lands a spot on *Jeopardy*, but manages to make a mess of his meeting with his hero Alex Trebec. Sam faces a disaster of his own: someone has stolen his little black book and is using it to turn his lady friends against him.

O. Episode One Hundred and Eighty

"Finally—Part One"

Written by Ken Levine and David Isaacs; Directed by James Burrows

Guest Starring: Roger Rees (Robin Colcord)

Rebecca finally has her way with Robin Colcord— or is it the other way around? Her date with Robin seems doomed when Robin invites Sam and a date along— but Sam is left behind when his date ditches him, and Rebecca finally realizes her dream. Sam decides to emulate Robin's technique to see if it will work for him, and takes his next date to the same restaurant that Robin took Rebecca to. . . only to find Robin there again with a different woman.

P. Episode One Hundred and Eighty Seven

"Finally—Part II"

Written by Ken Levine and David Isaacs; Directed by James Burrows

Guest Starring: Roger Rees (Robin Colcord), Bill Medley (Himself)

Robin tries to buy Sam's silence by giving him Cheers, but Sam can't keep from telling Rebecca the truth about Colcord. Rebecca refuses to accept the truth and waits in Robin's limousine, only to discover that Sam's words were true after all. But the smooth-talking Robin manages to sooth her anger, and gives her an expensive jewelled bracelet in the bargain.

Q. Episode One Hundred and Eighty Three

"Woody or Won't He?"

Written by Brian Pollack and Mert Rich; Directed by Andy Ackerman

Guest Starring: Jackie Swanson (Kelly Gaines), Melendy Britt (Roxanne Gaines), Richard Doyle (Mr. Gaines)

Woody meets Kelly's mother, who proceeds to come on to him. He finally rejects her in front of Kelly's entire family, and flees, embarrassed. Later, Kelly explains that everything is all right; her mother is really a harmless flirt. But the note of apology Woody gets from Kelly's mother is really another blatant attempt to get him into bed!

Meanwhile, Cliff has a harrowing encounter with a mechanical bull ride that cannot be turned off.

R. Episode One Hundred and Eighty Eight

"Severe Crane Damage"

Written by Dan O'Shannon and Tom Anderson; Directed by Andy Ackerman

Guest Starring: Phyllis Katz (Brenda Balzac)

Lilith has just published a new book, "Good Girls, Bad Boys," and appears on Brenda Balzac's talk show to promote it. Sam and Frasier go to the studio to watch and provide support. They wind up on stage, where the host gets Lilith to categorize the two men: Frasier is a "good" boy, while Sam is the "bad" boy. Needless to say, the all-woman audience finds Sam much more interesting, and Frasier is convinced that women find him boring. Determined to unleash his wild side, he takes up with Viper, a sinister female biker!

S. Episode One Hundred and Eighty Five

"Indoor Fun With Sammy and Robby"

Written by Phoef Sutton; Directed by Andy Ackerman

Guest Starring: Roger Rees (Robin Colcord)

Rebecca plans to spend a very full day with Robin, but Colcord gets involved in a darts game with Sam that soon escalates into a bitter rivalry. The Cheers team tries to help Sam beat Colcord at chess and are surprised when he manages to win on his own. . . but bad blood still prevails between the two men, and Rebecca doesn't get to spend any quality time with her dream man.

T. Episode One Hundred and Eighty Six

"Fifty-Fifty Carla"

Written by David Lloyd; Directed by James Burrows

Guest Starring: Roger Rees (Robin Colcord), Anne De Salvo (Gloria)

Carla decides to cheat Eddie LeBec's other widow, Gloria, out of a fifty-thousand dollar insurance settlement despite her promise to split everything fifty-fifty, and is soon consumed with guilt about her deception. Meanwhile, Woody lands a role in the play "Hair" only to become obsessed about the nudity in the play. Woody doesn't realize that this particular production does not involve any nudity, but his tension is so overwhelming that he strips on stage, even though everyone else remains fully clothed.

U. Episode One Hundred and Eighty Nine

"Bar Wars III: Return of Tecumseh"

Written by Ken Levine and David Isaacs; Directed by James Burrows

Cheers' wooden Indian mascot is missing, and only one person is nefarious enough to have made off with him: Sam's arch-rival Gary, of Gary's Old Towne Tavern. The guys retaliate by plastering Gary's bar with toxic waste warnings. Then they find out that Rebecca had removed the sculpture to have it cleaned and refinished. To forestall Gary's revenge, the men all shave their heads, except for Sam, who fakes it with a skull cap. The final blow falls with the revelation that Gary's Old Towne Tavern has been shut down for months!

V. Episode One Hundred and Ninety One

"Loverboyd"

Written by Brian Pollack and Mert Rich; Directed by James Burrows

Guest Starring: Jackie Swanson (Kelly Gaines), Richard Doyle (Mr. Gaines)

Kelly's father wants her to get Woody out of her mind, so he arranges for her to go off to school in Europe for a year. Woody and Kelly argue, and Woody decides to win her back and get her to elope with him. Being an old-fashioned guy at heart, Woody elopes the old-fashioned way: with a ladder at the window. When Kelly's father comes in, Woody hides in the closet, and what he overhears makes him realize that the father is acting out of love for his daughter, not out of malice towards Woody. He tells Kelly that he can't just take her away from her father in secret. Moved, Kelly agrees to be secretly engaged to Woody, a secret that will unite them while they are apart.

W. Episode One Hundred and Ninety Two

"The Ghost and Mrs. Lebec"

Written by Dan Stanley and Rob Long; Directed by James Burrows

Guest Starring: Georgia Brown (Madame Lazora)

Carla's plan to start dating again hits a bump of supernatural proportions when she is convinced that she is being haunted by the disapproving spirit of her dead husband, Eddie LeBec. She hires a medium, who is probably a fake, but the medium seems to make contact with Eddie, and Carla's mind is set at rest. Meanwhile, Rebecca gets involved in protesting a faulty ladies' ra-

zor, not realizing that it's made by Robin Colcord's company.

X. Episode One Hundred and Ninety

"Mr. Otis Regrets"

Written by Ken Levine and David Isaacs; Directed by Andy Ackerman

Rebecca determines to get the goods on her rival for Robin Colcord, and gets Sam to escort her to a social gala that her French rival will be attending. A bomb threat breaks up the soiree. Later, Sam claims that in the confusion he met the Frenchwoman, and that they had a steamy encounter in an elevator. If Rebecca knew her rival's sexual techniques, suggests the conniving Sam, she would stand a better chance in winning Colcord away from her. . . and who but Sam could reveal these secrets to Rebecca? Rebecca goes along with Sam's plan to recreate his imaginary tryst, only to turn the tables by securing Sam's hands, stripping him to his underwear, and leaving him to face the crowd on the ground floor.

NOTE: For those with short or no memories, the Otis of the title is the name of an elevator manufacturing company.

Y. Episode One Hundred and Ninety Three

"Cry Hard"

Written by Dan O'Shannon and Tom Anderson; Directed by James Burrows

Guest Starring: Roger Rees (Robin Colcord)

Robin Colcord finally gives in to Rebecca's charms and invites her to share his life. While they're off jetting about the globe, Norm, Woody, and Sam move her things into Colcord's home, only to uncover the awful truth: Colcord is using Rebecca to get insider information about the corporation that owns Cheers. While he's wining and dining her, his computer is tapping into the corporation's information banks. When Rebecca returns, it takes Sam a lot of persuading to accept the truth about Colcord, but finally they decide to unveil Colcord's backhanded maneuverings. But when Colcord shows up and asks Rebecca to marry him, she accepts!

Z. Episode One Hundred and Ninety Four

"Cry Harder"

Written by Cheri Eicehn, Bill Steinkellner and Phoef Sutton

Story by Bill Steinkellner; Directed by James Burrows

Guest Starring: Roger Rees (Robin Colcord)

Sam tries to convince the executives of the company that Rebecca is innocent of any wrongdoing, but that doesn't seem too convincing in the light of the fact that she's just run off with Colcord. Sam exposes Colcord's guilt; Colcord is arrested, but soon is free on a two-million dollar bail bond. To show their gratitude to Sam, the corporation sells the bar back to him for one dollar. Everyone is overjoyed except Rebecca, who is furious to learn that Sam turned Colcord in. She still plans to marry Colcord anyway, but these plans cave in when government agents announce that Colcord has fled the country. Rebecca receives a fax from Colcord confirming this.

Crushed, she decides to stay on at Cheers as a waitress, and finally flings herself at Sam after the bar closes. Suddenly, Colcord barges in, only to find Sam and Rebecca in bed in the bar's

office!

SEASON NINE

(1990-1991)

Kirstie Alley and Rhea Perlman

A. Episode One Hundred and Ninety Six

"Love Is A Really, Really Perfectly Okay Thing"

Sam and Rebecca, caught in bed by Robin Colcord, deny that they've done anything even remotely sexual. Colcord explains that he's changed his mind about fleeing the country, and plans to turn himself in. Rebecca decides to stick by Colcord, but stays as a waitress at Cheers. Tension between her and Sam is quite noticeable. Meanwhile, the gang expects Sam to spill the beans about his big evening with Rebecca, provoking a crisis of conscience for Sam.

B. Episode One Hundred and Ninety Five

"Cheers Fouls Out"

Sam cons his pal, Celtics star Kevin McHale, into being a "ringer" in the annual basketball game against Gary's Old Towne Tavern by telling McHale that its a charity game for orphans. When the truth comes out, Sam has to promise McHale that he'll donate the prize money to a local orphanage. With the pro's assistance, Cheers wins the game— but Woody accidentally causes McHale to twist his ankle.

Later, the bar's big party is interrupted by the team doctor of the Celtics. It seems that McHale's injury will keep him from playing for the rest of the year. A frantic Carla bribes the doctor with the five-thousand dollars won in the basketball game so that no one will find out that Cheers was involved. When McHale shows up, however, he's not injured at all, and Carla begins to smell a rat. Sure enough, Gary shows up and donates five thousand dollars to

the orphanage in the name of his establishment; the doctor was a fake, and Cheers has been duped again.

C. Episode One Hundred and Ninety Seven

"Rebecca Redux"

Sam hires an old pal to help run the bar but realizes that he needs Rebecca's help. But Rebecca has gone on to bigger, if not necessarily better, things: she represents a brand of car wax at trade shows. Sam needs to save her from this desperate career move and get her back at the bar. But his friend is a hit with the Cheers gang, and they don't want Rebecca back. Sam's friend proves to be a gentleman, however, and Rebecca returns, while Sam devises a way to smooth the ruffled feathers of the regulars.

D. Episode One Hundred and Ninety Eight

"Where Nobody Knows Your Name"

The Robin Colcord case has generated a lot of media excitement, fuelled by the fact that Colcord turned himself in for the woman he loved.

Rebecca keeps a low profile, but her French rival Jeanne Marie does not, taking the credit for Colcord's change of heart and basking in all the attention, which includes a guest spot on "Arsenio." Rebecca tries to keep cool about this but finally gives in to anger and confusion. She sends Sam to find out what Colcord's real feelings are. When Sam explains things to the corporate raider at his luxurious upstate prison, Colcord calls the media to say that it was Rebecca, not Jeanne Marie, that he loved. But the media, having burned out on the issue, doesn't even deem this to be newsworthy.

E. Episode One Hundred and Ninety Nine

"Ma Always Liked You Best"

When Cliff Clavin, giddy with independence, declines to have his mother live with him, Mrs. Clavin winds up staying with Woody, who becomes her surrogate son! Jealousy soon enters Cliff's heart, and he and Woody argue over her until she declares that they should act like brothers, since she cares for them both.

F. Episode Two Hundred and One

"Grease"

Guest cast: Sheldon Leonard (Sid Nelson)

The Hungry Heifer, Norm Peterson's favorite eatery, is going to be demolished. Norm circulates a petition and is able to get the restaurant declared a landmark. But Sid, the owner, is unhappy with this development because he stands to get a lot of money for his property. He also feels guilty about all the unhealthy, greasy food he's fed people for so long. Finally he tries to burn the building down, while a frantic Norm tries to dissuade him.

G. Episode Two Hundred and Seven

"Breaking In Is Hard To Do"

Rebecca goes to incredible lengths to get intimate with Robin Colcord, eventually breaking into his prison— only to be turned down so as not to jeopardize his parole standing!

H. Episodes Two Hundred and Two/Three

"Anniversary Show"

Guest host: John McLaughlin (Himself)

Celebrating the two-hundredth episode of Cheers ("Bad Neighbor Sam"), Shelley Long reunites with the current cast for a Q & A session moderated by the doughty John McLaughlin. Series highlights are reviewed, and Nicholas Colasanto is remembered, in this hour-long double episode.

I. Episode Two Hundred

"Bad Neighbor Sam"

Guest cast: Keene Curtis (John Allen Hill), Thomas W. Babson (Himself)

Melville's, the posh restaurant directly upstairs from Cheers, has a new owner who has turned the place into a chic, upscale eatery whose clients act like Cheers is nothing but Melville's waiting room. To make matters worse, the new owner John Allen Hill claims Sam's parking space and has Sam's Corvette towed away. . . and walls off the poolroom and restroom of Cheers which, according to his lease, belong to him. Sam begins to veer into mental instability, and the regulars start a betting pool as to when he will finally blow his top! Sam finally snaps when he is faced with the fact that he'll have to rent the pool room and bathrooms from Hill. . . who wins the pool by correctly guessing the time of Sam's big blowout!

EPISODES

122

J. Episode Two Hundred and Four

"Veggie-Boyd"

Woody lands a professional acting gig, in a commercial for the "Veggie-Boy" drink. The whole gang watches the advertisement's television debut, and toast Woody with a glass of the product. . . Woody discovers that Veggie-Boy tastes awful. He is so disturbed to have represented the product that he totally loses his composure, and Frasier must help him by hypnotizing him, in the hopes that he can make Woody like the taste after all.

K. Episode Two Hundred and Five

"Norm and Cliff's Excellent Adventure"

Norm and Cliff reminisce about their youthful days of pulling pranks on their friends, and decide to relive the past by engineering conflicts between the Cheers regulars. They play a trick on Frasier by reporting his credit card as being stolen while Frasier and Lilith are hosting a psychiatric party at the bar. When Sam tries to ring up Frasier's sizeable tab on the card, the charge cannot go through, and Sam must cut the "stolen" credit card in half. Frasier becomes furious at Sam and threatens to shun the bar for the rest of his life. Norm and Cliff are good at jokes, but setting matters right between Sam and Frasier doesn't turn out to be as easy as starting the trouble in the first place.

L. Episode Two Hundred and Eight

"Woody Interruptus"

Guest cast: Jackie Swanson (Kelly Gaines), Anthony Cistero (Henri)

While Cliff ponders the idea of having his head cryogenically frozen (hopefully not while he's still alive, though), Kelly Gaines returns from France at last, but Woody's joy is undercut by the presence of her French photography teacher, who obviously has designs on Woody's gal. Sam suggests that all it'll take to make Kelly forget the French guy is a night of sex at a good hotel, especially after Woody reveals that he and Kelly have kept their relationship platonic so far.

Woody rents a motel room, and Kelly goes along with the idea, but they come to the conclusion that they should let their relationship develop first, and that a better hotel room might help matters as well.

M. Episode Two Hundred and Six

"Honor Thy Mother"

Guest cast: Keene Curtis (John Allen Hill), Sada Thompson (Mama Lozupone),

Josh Lazoff (Gino Tortelli)

Carla's mother, known as Mama, senses that her end is near, and reveals her final wish to her daughter. It seems a simple continuation of a family tradition that requires one of Carla's male children to take the maiden name of Mama's mother and the family name of her father. Unfortunately, this will produce the unfortunate appellation of Benito Mussolini, the name of Italy's Fascist dictator from the 1920's through World War Two. Carla is less than pleased when her son Gino likes the idea. . . and thinks "Il Duce" is a great nickname!

N. Episode Two Hundred and Nine

"Achilles Hill"

Guest cast: Keene Curtis (John Allen Hill), Valerie Mahaffey (Pamela Hill)

Sam decides to get back at Hill by dating his daughter, who goes along with the idea simply as a means of rebelling against her father. Hill plays it cool but finally breaks down and offers Sam free use of the disputed back rooms if he'll stop dating Pamela. Sam agrees, but reneges when he discovers that he really likes the charming young woman. His efforts to keep this a secret from Hill fail, but Hill is genuinely calm at the revelation, revealing that he is willing to let her daughter make her own decisions. When Pamela discovers that her father is not opposed to her dating Sam, her reason for going out with Sam dissipates, and she dumps him. Hill gets the last laugh by doubling the rent on the disputed room, leaving Sam fuming.

O. Episode Two Hundred and Ten

"Days of Wine and Neuroses"

Robin Colcord proposes to Rebecca again, this time by mail from his prison. The whole Cheers gang celebrates, but the proceeding takes on a sour note when Frasier becomes enamored of the new Karaoke machine (an electronic device that allows people to sing along to backing tracks of popular songs) and drives everyone crazy with his off key singing. As Rebecca gets drunker, she begins to question her feelings for Robin.

Worried about Rebecca, Sam follows her home to check up on her. Completely sloshed, she reveals that she doesn't love Robin— she craves Sam Malone! Continuing the evening's trend of bad vocalizing, she sings "We've Got Tonight" to Sam before collapsing in a drunken stupor in his arms.

P. Episode Two Hundred and Eleven

"Wedding Bell Blues"

Guest cast: Bobby Hatfield (Himself)

The day following the events of "Days of Wine and Neuroses" dawns with Rebecca completely unaware of what she had said to Sam. She denies it completely, but Sam realizes— and not only for selfish reasons— that he has to sabotage the wedding. Righteous Brother Bobby Hatfield is scheduled to sing "Unchained Melody" (which will always date this episode to the year of *Ghost*) at the ceremony, but Sam switches the ever-present Karaoke machine to "We've Got Tonight," and Rebecca's memory is restored. She runs away, returns, and decides to go ahead with the wedding anyway. . . only to run away again, leaving Colcord alone at the altar.

Q. Episode Two Hundred and Twelve"

"I'm Getting My Act Together and Sticking It In Your Face"

After holing up in Sam's office for several days, a frazzled Rebecca borrows Woody's car and drives to the airport, where she heads for her old hometown, San Diego. After two weeks pass with no word from her, Sam calls her parents and leaves a message from the whole gang, saying that they love her. But Sam accidentally (?) says "I" instead of "we," which leads him to panic when he discovers that Rebecca is hurrying back to be with him.

R. Episode Two Hundred and Fourteen

"Sam Time Next Year"

Guest cast: Barbara Feldon (Lauren Hudson)

Sam hurts his back in a fall, but he's determined to keep his traditional Valentine's Day date with his old flame Lauren. He enlists Woody to drive him to Vermont for the annual reunion. Woody discreetly fades from view in order to keep from spoiling Sam's romantic evening, and spends a long, cold night outside their cabin, only to discover in the morning that Sam's injury made passion impossible— and the two old lovers merely talked all night.

S. Episode Two Hundred and Thirteen

"Crash of the Titans"

Guest cast: Keene Curtis (John Allen Hill)

Rebecca wants to buy Cheers from Sam. When he scoffs at the idea, she rents the disputed back rooms from John Allen Hill for a price a great deal higher than what Sam was paying for them. Soon, Hill is thrilled to have the two of them trying to outbid each other, but things take a sour turn when Rebecca tries to use her feminine wiles to get Hill to sell to her— and Hill expects her to come across. Fortunately, Sam rescues her from this fate worse than death, and they make up and decide to buy the room from Hill as partners.

T. Episode Two Hundred and Fifteen

"It's A Wonderful Wife"

Guest Cast: Anthony Cistero (Henri Fourchette), Keene Curtis (John Allen Hill), Bernadette Birkett (Voice of Vera)

When Norm's wife Vera loses her job, Rebecca helps her get a job as a hat check girl upstairs at Melville's. This puts a bit of a damper on Mr. Peterson's ability to have fun at Cheers— so he goes home to clean house instead. But when Hill fires Vera, the Peterson pride is aroused, leading to a showdown with Hill.

U. Episode Two Hundred and Sixteen

"Cheers Has Chili"

Rebecca's plan to convert the pool room meets with Sam's mockery, and he bets her that she won't be able to earn one thousand dollars a week with this crazy idea. Sam's doubts seem well founded until Woody starts dishing out his own homemade chili in the back room. A jealous Sam tips off the Fire Marshall about an unauthorized kitchen on the premises— but when the Marshal shows up, all he wants is a copy of the recipe, and Sam finally admits defeat.

V. Episode Two Hundred and Eighteen

"Carla Loves Clavin"

Cliff tricks Carla into believing that he's a judge in the city-wide barmaid contest, which drives Carla to the unpleasant task of being nice to the annoying mailman. When she discovers the truth, her rage drives her to outperform all the other competitors— only to see a clumsy but cute contestant awarded the prize by the lecherous real judge. Needless to say, Cliff Clavin is in for a taste of hell as only Carla can serve it up!

W. Episode Two Hundred and Seventeen

"Pitch It Again, Sam"

Guest cast: Michael Fairman (Dutch Kincaid), Henry Woronicz (Rick Casper)

Dutch Kincaid is an old baseball rival of Sam's who Sam could never strike out. When Kincaid asks him to pitch at a game in Kincaid's honor, Sam takes on the challenge of finally shutting out the man. But when a kid claiming to be Kincaid's grandson begs Sam for a chance to see one of Dutch's legendary grand slams, Sam gives Dutch a home run— after throwing two perfect strikes. Of course no one believes he did it intentionally— and Sam sees red when he learns that Kincaid's "grandson" was really the son of the event's promoter!

X. Episode Two Hundred and Nineteen

"Rat Girl"

Guest cast: Paul Wilson (Paul), Beth Toussaint (Paula)

Frasier has unusual domestic difficulties when Lilith begins to act a bit peculiar. . . it seems that she's been driven over the edge by the death of her favorite laboratory rat!

Y. Episode Two Hundred and Twenty

"Home Malone"

Guest Cast: Jackie Swanson (Kelly Gains), Anthony Cistero (Henri Fourchette)

While Kelly gets the full Carla treatment as a trainee waitress as Cheers, Sam babysits for Lilith and Frasier, only to find himself locked out of the house. This provokes a series of comic attempts to get back before Frasier and Lilith get back.

Z. Episode Two Hundred and Twenty One

"Uncle Sam Wants You"

Guest Cast: Peta Wilcox (Elvis), Paul Wilson (Paul)

Sam begins to spend so much time with young Frederick , Frasier's son, that the parents eventually ask him to leave. Hurt, Sam realizes that he likes children, and wonders about having one of his own. He begins to ask almost every woman he meets, winning him more than a few slaps and put-downs— only to have Rebecca Howe agree to help him out in his quest for parenthood!

Rhea Perlman
as Carla Tortelli

Kirstie Alley and Ted Danson

THE FUTURE: SEASON TEN

Unlike many tribute books, this present volume chronicles a series still very much alive. As such the author is forced to give only a brief glimpse at the tenth season, currently airing as this is written, knowing full well that things will change before his words see print.

*T*he tenth year of *Cheers* started off by picking up the cliffhanger of season nine involving Sam and Rebecca deciding to have a baby. While the first two episodes dealt with this, it became obvious that what seemed a great idea the previous spring had been reconsidered by summer, possibly due to *Murphy Brown* introducing a major running subplot about her being pregnant, the producers and writers of *Cheers* probably decided to veer away from this angle since it would no longer appear as unique. This was probably a wise idea for a number of reasons as longtime fans of *Murphy Brown* have not exactly greeted the impending motherhood of Murphy with open arms. Since Sam is as individualistic in his own right as Murphy, the concept of fatherhood for Sam Malone might also have seemed incongruous if it actually happened.

What the show did do was make it clear that Sam and Rebecca were trying very hard to conceive, but without success. Along the way Sam babysits for Frasier and Lilith and the baby makes a monkey out of him. Sam twice is locked out of the bathroom by the child and when he climbs outside the window to get to the bathroom, is accidentally locked out of the apartment. He has to jump to the ground in order to re-enter the building.

Sam and Rebecca both decide to baby-sit Carla's kids to see what it is really like to have a family. The result is horrific as they discover that Carla's kids are just as demonic as she'd always claimed. In this episode Rebecca starts having second thoughts about motherhood.

For several episodes, the motherhood angle is dropped as stories focus on other characters . The guys all decided to drive out west to get in touch with their manhood, but the car breaks down in the middle of the desert - although it turns out to be just over the hill from a lavish resort.

The annual Halloween feud with Gary's Goodtime Tavern explodes in a strange episode in which Gary has a heart attack due to a complex stunt involving a hologram projected into the bar. we believe he was dead right up until the climax when it's revealed that Carla and the others concocted the stunt with Gary to fool Sam. What made this work is that even Sam thinks it's a trick and keeps insisting that none of it is true, even in the face of seemingly incontrovertible evidence. By the time he is convinced, so are we, which is when the truth is unveiled. It demonstrates that the writing on *Cheers* remains as sharp as ever.

Carla has a bizarre episode centered around her when she has an affair with the owner of the restaurant above Cheers, a hateful man who has been giving Sam a hard time since season 9. When Sam discovers that Carla has slept with him, he feels betrayed. It's an odd episode, right up until the end.

Woody's relationship with his girlfriend is revived when she is almost tricked into marrying the recurring French character who constantly boasts about how he is going to steal Woody's girl away from her. There is a very funny sequence when first Sam, and then Woody, rush to City Hall and interrupt the same wedding ceremony, mistaking it for Kelly's wedding. When the scheme is exposed, Kelly refuses to go through with the marriage and the impression is left that she and Woody may well wed one day. For a time there was talk of just writing Kelly's character out of the show entirely, but the thinking on this has changed.

Throwaway gags galore still dot the episodes, such as Carla asking, for no particular reason, "What I want to know is, if the Brady Bunch crash in the Himalayas, who do they eat first?"

The question of Sam and Rebecca's planned child is posed again after several episodes in which it wasn't mentioned. When Rebecca insists that Sam have his sperm count tested, he regards even the question as an assault on his manhood. But when Rebecca's fertility tests positive, the question remains that she may not have conceived because of Sam. Interwoven with this is a subplot involving Lilith making out her will and wanting Frasier to do the same. He resists but then agrees. In the end, when Sam returns with the envelope containing his test results, he refuses to look at them because he has that much faith in himself. The envelope gets switched with the one containing Frasier's will and in an odd epilogue, the episode ends with a "Many years later" tag in which Lilith is attending the reading of Frasier's will and the attorney opens the envelope and reads, "Sam Malone's sperm count is well above average," to which Lilith responds, "That damn bar!"

The question of Sam and Rebecca having a child is finally put to rest when they realize that they've been wanting to have a child for all the wrong reasons, and that whenever either of them has a child, it should be because they love each other and want to have a family. By putting the issue to rest in this way, it is in a sense a slap at the way *Murphy Brown* is handling the issue. She became pregnant by chance instead of by design and chose not to marry the biological father because neither of them could handle the prospect of marriage again. Thus the child will grow up without having a normal two parent family. I think that *Cheers* handled the issue much better, addressing the fact that people should have children for reasons which are beneficial to the child, not for selfish reasons of the parent. Sam and Rebecca initially wanted to have a child because they liked being around Frasier and Lilith's baby and wanted to have one of their own, almost as though they were talking about a new VCR rather than a child. Their decision not to have a child until the circumstances would be the best for the child as well as the most mature decision.

While season ten of *Cheers* was for a time rumored to be the last, Ted Danson has confirmed that this is not the case. There will be at least an eleventh season, and as long as the cast continues to enjoy making the show, the show will probably continue. Certainly the writing shows no signs of sagging or falling into familiar patterns the way it does on the less adventurous sitcoms which clutter the channels.